Sanctuary Secrets

to personal prayer

Books by Carrol Johnson Shewmake:

Practical Pointers to Personal Prayer
Sanctuary Secrets to Personal Prayer
Sensing His Presence, Hearing His Voice
What to Say (with Daniel O'Ffill)
When We Pray for Others
The Worshiping Heart
The Many Faces of God

For order information about this new version of *Sanctuary Secrets to Personal Prayer,* email the author at cjshewmake@prayerpartners.com

Sanctuary Secrets

to personal prayer

Revised and Expanded

Carrol Johnson Shewmake

This book was edited by John Shewmake, Sr.
Copyedited by Jean Bartling
Cover design: Donna Orth
Technical advisor: John Shewmake, Jr.

PRINTED IN U.S.A.

Eau Claire Printing Company
415 Galloway Street
Eau Claire, Wisconsin 54703
www.ecprinting.com

ISBN 0-9767705-0-4

Dedication

I lovingly dedicate the rewrite of this book to the following people:

To my husband John who always has an encouraging word and who never lets me give up.

To Michael and Carol who introduced me to Sanctuary Prayer many years ago.

To the readers of my books and the participants in my seminars, whose wholehearted response encourages me to keep on writing and speaking.

To Jean Bartling who shares my heart-cry for God, and who gave generously of her time to read this manuscript to keep me on track with grammar and punctuation.

Contents

Introduction

The title of this book, *Sanctuary Secrets to Personal Prayer*, may sound familiar to you. A book by that title has been around since 1990. I wrote it as a handbook to explain Sanctuary Prayer when I began speaking at women's retreats, campmeetings, and individual churches about prayer. It was a companion to my first book, *Practical Pointers to Personal Prayer*, which told my personal prayer story. The people who heard me speak could take these books home to study and help them grow in intimacy with God.

But last year my publisher decided it was time to retire some of my books—they had been in print much longer than average—and *Sanctuary Secrets* was the first to go. However, I've had so many requests for *Sanctuary Secrets* since then that I am reprinting it, revised and enlarged to flesh out the message.

I have told much of my personal story in my book *Practical Pointers to Personal Prayer* (Review and Herald

Publishing Assn.). Yet frequently readers of that book request more information about Sanctuary Prayer.

"I loved your book," a friend who lives across the continent confided to me on a recent visit. "Yet I did have one disappointment."

"What was that?" I asked.

"Well, in the few quiet moments we've had together on our visits, you've told me bits and pieces about sanctuary prayer, and my heart has responded. I had hoped that you would put all those pieces together for me in your book. After I had completed the book I even went back and searched to see if I had overlooked something. But it just isn't there. I want to know more about Sanctuary Prayer."

So in this book my focus will be on what we call Sanctuary Prayer. God hears every honest prayer and there is no magic formula for prayer, yet I've found that having a growing knowledge of what God wants me to talk to Him about makes me more conscious of His presence in my prayer time and in my life. And that is what Sanctuary Prayer does for me.

People have asked me over the years what the special appeal of the sanctuary is for me. After all, blood sacrifices and all those sanctuary rituals are terribly distasteful in this modern age. In this book I will share the *real* story of the purpose of the sanctuary and its meaning for us today. No, I'm not attracted by the blood sacrifices—but I'm ever so grateful for the blood sacrifice of Jesus who died and rose to life again that I might have eternal life. To me that blood has a very sweet aroma. And it is that sacrifice and that blood that every animal killed for a sacrifice to God in the sanctuary services until the death of Christ, has represented.

We may wonder why the constant reminders, repeated over and over and over again throughout the hundreds and thousands of years before Christ came to earth, were necessary. Did God delight in the death of all of those innocent animals? Surely God, who notices when even a sparrow falls to the earth, does not enjoy death—even of an animal. I believe He sorrowed for every animal sacrifice.

God explained in the scriptures that life is in the blood (Leviticus 17:11). Blood contains the physical elements of life. *But only the blood of Jesus contains eternal life.* God knew that placing bloody death within humanity's worship experience was the best way to remind human beings of the enormity of sin, its dreadful consequences and the cost required for salvation. Human beings are so hard of hearing and understanding that it often takes dramatic measures to catch our attention. But God loves us so much that He is willing to do whatever it takes to accomplish this task. He is not willing that *any* should be eternally lost without having the opportunity to accept salvation. The Jewish nation was to be representative of God's plan for the entire world, not just the Israelites.

The wilderness sanctuary story is filled with meaning for us even today. It is the gospel hidden away in the Old Testament—promise of a coming Redeemer, the same God who has been involved with mankind since the world was created:

- Promise of His coming to earth to live as one of us and offer the sacrifice to end all sacrifices
- Promise of His continual presence with us in this world of sin

iii

- Promise of the end of sin and the beginning of eternal life

Yes, the sanctuary illustration still has meaning for us today. Studied together with the life of Christ, it gives us insight into God's plan for erasing sin from the universe. It shows us why Jesus had to die and gives us hope of eternal life. The line of Bible prophecies would be incomplete without the sanctuary illustration.

But the greatest blessing I have personally received from the sanctuary is the reality of God's personal involvement with me. Yes, God is interested in everything about me. He desires an intimate love relationship with *me*.

CHAPTER ONE

God Loves to Share
His Secrets with Us!

*"Call to me and I will answer you
and tell you great and unsearchable
things you do not know."
(Jeremiah 33:3)*

Have you ever wondered about God's secrets?
Deuteronomy 29:29 tells us: "The secret things
belong to the Lord our God, but the things revealed
belong to us and to our children forever, that we may
follow all the words of this law."

There are secret things which belong only to God. No
way can we understand them. God is eternal, immortal,
omniscient—how could mortals possibly comprehend all
that God has in His mind? These are sacred secrets
known only to God the Father, God the Son, and God the
Holy Spirit.

1

But the Bible is filled with secrets God *has* revealed. These He is longing to share with us. How can we discover them? We know the answer to that question: Bible study and prayer. Yet often we spend years reading the Bible and praying, yet learning little. Why is that?

As I began to realize that the Bible was filled with secrets I did not know—and did not know how to find—I began claiming the promise of Jeremiah 33:3 quoted at the beginning of this chapter. (God loves to have us ask for the things the Bible promises us!)

In this book I want to share with you keys God showed me for discovering His hidden secrets. These secrets cannot be found by simply reading the Bible through or memorizing key texts about doctrinal beliefs, profitable as these both are. God desires us to search for His secrets as if we were looking for hidden treasure. The illustration God gave Moses in the wilderness sanctuary is a map to rich treasure.

In the books of Exodus and Leviticus Moses has recorded the story of how God directed Moses to lead a vast company of his relatives, all descendents of Abraham, but now slaves, from Egypt to Caanan. God had promised Abraham that He would make a great nation of his descendents. God would be their God and they would be His special people.

But as a nation they did not seem promising. They had ended up in slavery in Egypt, and as a result they were ignorant, rebellious, quarrelsome and desperate. The years of slavery had nearly wiped out the memory of the promise handed down from father to son since Adam[1] which promised that a Redeemer would be born into the human race. He would redeem mankind from the

2

judgment of death, cleanse the world of rebellion, and rule in peace.

By a series of astounding miracles, God used Moses to lead the Israelites out of slavery in Egypt and on their way to the promised land of Caanan. As they camped around Mt.Sinai at the beginning of their journey, God gave Moses a vision of heaven and God's glorious holy temple there.

"Now, Moses," God said, "I want you to build a portable model of the temple you have seen in vision. I will give you the exact dimensions you are to use and instructions for how to go about building this sanctuary."

In God's own words (as transcribed by Moses) God said: "Then have them make a sanctuary for me, and I will dwell among them. Make this tabernacle and all its furnishings exactly like the pattern I will show you" (Exodus 25:8, 9).

Have you ever wondered how it was possible for the many generations before the birth of Jesus to understand the loving character of God? The slaves Moses led away from Egypt were illiterate, ungodly, ignorant. How was it possible for them to comprehend the true God?

The Israelites had seen God at work as He had pressed the ruler of Egypt to allow them to leave. They recognized His mighty power. But God longed for them to see his love. Each miracle He performed for them as they traveled through the desert was to increase their love and respect for Him.

But God had a more comprehensive plan. It was simple and it was beautiful. He asked Moses to build an earthly model of God's heavenly work in their behalf that they could be involved with. Miracles were great—the people loved them! But God wanted the people to catch a glimpse of heaven's work on behalf of sinners. He wanted them to understand the enormity of sin and the price necessary to forgive sin. He wanted to show them that He not only loved them but that He wanted *an intimate relationship* with them. He wanted to be intimately involved in their lives. In this model He would come to dwell among them. The sanctuary Moses built and its services would hold the revealed secrets of God and His dealings with all mankind throughout the rest of earth time.

God desired that the Israelites would not only see Him in the glory that would fill this sanctuary but that they would also see *an illustration of how He planned to save each one of them.* Each article of furniture, each ritual sacrifice, each act of service performed in the sanctuary was to point forward to the promised Redeemer and the divine plan for salvation.

But what about the rest of the world? Would God save only the Jews? Were they the only ones He loved?

It was God's plan that as His people took their place in the land He had given them at the crossroads of the then-known world, they would become teachers of righteousness. Travelers passing through Israel would be attracted to the one God who cares for all people. They would then scatter the story of salvation throughout their travels. Thus the whole world would come to know Him. Had His people been faithful this would have been the story.

Often it is only through hardship, trial, or sorrow that humans are able to step out in faith to know God better. It was that way with the Israelites. It was that way with me:

4

My husband and I faced the greatest trial of our lives, estrangement from someone we dearly loved. Although my husband and I were in this together, we seemed to face our grief alone. Panic engulfed me in hopelessness. I, who had been a leader in prayer, suddenly had a hard time praying. God seemed far away. "Help!" was the only word I could find to pray. Darkness surrounded me. Joy was only a dim memory. I felt I had not only lost my loved one, but I had lost my God.

In desperation I began to seek out every gathering where people came together to pray. One afternoon I was in a prayer group led by a young Jewish man who was a member of the church my husband pastored. He told us how, as a youth raised as a strict Jew, he had studied the sanctuary and its services. He said that when he became a born-again Christian he was surprised to find that in every part of the sanctuary building and in every sacrifice and ministry connected with it, he saw Jesus. Jesus was the Sacrifice, Jesus was the High Priest.

Then this young man made a statement that penetrated through my darkness into my grief-clouded mind, *"God had Moses build the sanctuary in the wilderness to show how God saves each human soul."*

I had been raised in the church, had attended church schools, I was married to a minister, and I read and studied my Bible. But I had looked at the wilderness sanctuary story simply as history, prophecy, and doctrine. I vaguely understood that the sanctuary service pointed to the time of the Redeemer's birth—but somehow it had never entered my mind that it had any *personal* meaning for me.

The young man went on to say that he had been blessed by taking the steps of the priests in their sanctuary work as a guide for his morning prayers. He explained how the priests came into the courtyard of the sanctuary each morning to begin their daily ministry, chanting or singing praises to God. They offered a sacrifice for the sins of the people on the bronze altar representing the cross of Calvary, washed in the bronze basin representing baptism, entered the first apartment of the sanctuary where the light of the seven-branched lampstand, representing the Holy Spirit, needed daily care to keep the light burning continually. Across the room a table held twelve loaves of bread which represented the life and blood of the coming Redeemer. The priest sprinkled some of the blood from the sacrifice, accompanied by sweet incense, upon the golden altar. The incense wafted over the curtain into the Most Holy Place, God's designated dwelling place on earth. The only article of furniture in the Most Holy Place was a very special chest called the ark; inside the ark were the stone tablets upon which God Himself had engraved the Ten Commandments. The ark was covered by the mercy seat, God's special place of rest. The glory of God was visible to the entire camp in the pillar of light by night and the sheltering cloud by day.

Of course, the young man did not say exactly the words I have written—but this is the picture I carried away from this meeting—the picture of a way to personally connect with God—to understand Him better. It was definitely a miracle of grace that, in my distraught condition, I was able to hold that picture in my heart and mind. I grabbed the sanctuary illustration like a drowning person grabs at anything to save his life. Perhaps an outline like this would give me more than one word to pray.

I was eager to communicate with God.

I began praying through the sanctuary the next morning. The miracle was real. Gone was the darkness and guilt. I sensed God's presence in my prayer time. I had no trouble finding words to pray. God began to talk to me through scripture and the inward voice of the Holy Spirit in a way I had seldom experienced before. Instead of looking at my problem, I began to look at God.

The surprise for me was that God did not address my current problem but reached into my inmost heart and began pointing out the areas in my life that needed change—all the while assuring me of His presence in my life.

"I will never leave you—never—never," He promised.

A second surprise was that I welcomed God's discipline. It was as though I realized that if God would take the time to correct me He surely hadn't given up on me! There must be an answer to my problem. For the first time in weeks I found joy.

A third surprise was my immediate response to share with others the work being done in my life   I called friends together on a Friday evening in our home. My joy and enthusiasm were contagious, and others began to hope that God would do the same for them. It was definitely revival time in my life and in the lives of those around me. It was a dramatic change. No wonder I talk about Sanctuary Prayer! My prayer life was changed overnight, never to go back into the same darkness. Since then I have met others who remember the day, the hour, when they began Sanctuary Prayer, for it had the same dramatic result in their lives.

I am not asking everyone to pray just like I do! I may sound like that because I am still excited about what God is teaching me daily through Sanctuary Prayer after almost 20 years. However, I realize that we don't all have to pray alike. We are each individuals and God loves our individuality.

God's ministry for us never differs from His original plan of redemption. He is still seeking His people in the same ways. As God made Himself visible to the Israelites through the ministry of the priests in the earthly sanctuary, as Jesus made God visible while He ministered here on earth, so today God wants to become visible to us as we seek Him in the Heavenly Sanctuary. The same seven steps of the earthly priests that made God visible to the people of Israel will teach us, modern Israel, the things that are important today in our relationship with God—His great plans for us.

We must remember that the sanctuary we are considering today is *not* the earthly sanctuary Moses built in the wilderness, nor the temple in Jerusalem which was destroyed thousands of years ago. We are using the illustration of the sanctuary in the way God planned for it to be used—as a visual aid to understand Christ's ministry in the *Heavenly Sanctuary*. Our focus today is on God's true sanctuary which is in heaven.

We are not looking back to relive the past but eagerly accepting the present and looking *upward* to the heavenly sanctuary where God is still guiding the destiny of His people, looking backward only to glimpse the cross and the lessons God has for us. (*These last two paragraphs are so important that I suggest you reread them before you go on with the rest of the book!*)

God has "great and unsearchable things" He longs to teach us (Jeremiah 33:3). He is limited only by our *not seeking, not asking, and not understanding.*

Things Sanctuary Prayer did for me immediately:

- It gave me *something to talk to God about* (took away panic)—
- It *focused* my mind first of all on praising God. And then the cross—
- It *took away my guilt* as I confessed specific sins and accepted specific forgiveness— I was *forgiven*—
- It kept *order* in my prayers—it gave me *boundaries*—
- Rather than getting stuck on a single word I *progressed* on to another part of my prayer—
- When I had finished my prayer I felt *complete,* wholly accepted by God—*peace* in my heart—the *bright glow of hope*—a light which has never gone out.

That was the *immediate result* of Sanctuary Prayer. The long range results were just as dramatic. God embarked me upon a learning program that I hope will never end. He began teaching me those "great and unsearchable things I did not know" (Jeremiah 33:3). This He promises to do for all those who call upon Him in prayer, earnestly seeking knowledge and understanding.

Sanctuary Prayer is not the only prayer I pray daily. It's true that I usually begin my day praying through the sanctuary but throughout the day and night I pray many short prayers: prayers of praise, rededication, intercession for others, cries for help, protection, forgiveness, wisdom. And I pray with others as often as possible, short prayers, conversational prayers. I pray on the telephone, while I am at work, as I visit. But Sanctuary Prayer has guided me in study, teaching me about God, about righteousness by faith. It is a teaching tool, leading me always to intimacy with the great Teacher!

The purpose of this book is to lead you step by step through a unique prayer, following the footsteps of the Israelite priests in their sanctuary ministry. As I do this I will share with you how the plan of salvation is delineated in the ministries of the earthly sanctuary and how Christ's daily work for us today in the heavenly sanctuary is made clear through the sanctuary illustration. Because the only firsthand knowledge I have of this prayer is my own personal experience, I can only relate to you how I daily seek to cooperate with Jesus in this work. I pray that this personal glimpse will prove inspirational to you and be God-centered rather than self-centered and that you will find courage and faith to begin your own search for God's secrets.

SUMMARY

There are secret things which belong only to God. Of God's eternal qualities and the vastness of His universe, we can only occasionally catch glimpses.

But the Bible is filled with secrets God has revealed and is longing to share with us (Jeremiah 33:3). The Bible, of course, is the storehouse of God's revealed secrets but must be studied under the guidance of the Holy Spirit to discover them.

God has given us, in the Old Testament sanctuary and its ministries and sacrifices, an outline of the entire scope of His redemptive work for the world from the time Adam and Eve sinned until the second coming of Jesus. Every part of the sanctuary service pointed to Jesus, our Redeemer, and shows us His ministry—what He accomplished for us when he came to earth as a man, and also what He is doing for us now in the Heavenly Sanctuary to make the universe safe from sin for eternity.

This outline includes history, prophecy, and doctrine. But first and foremost for the individual it contains the promise that *God had Moses build the sanctuary in the wilderness to show how He saves each human soul.*

Following the footsteps of the priests as they performed their service in the earthly sanctuary, gives us an outline of the secrets of God's redemptive plan. Using this outline for my daily morning prayers has led me into greater intimacy with God than I had ever imagined was possible.

As we study the work of the earthly priests, we must always remember that the wilderness sanctuary was just a model, an illustration, of what God is actually doing in heaven and in our hearts. Always we must look upward to the Heavenly Sanctuary.

---

[1] Genesis 3:15

CHAPTER TWO

Enter His Gates
With Praise

*"Enter his gates with thanksgiving and his courts with praise;
give thanks to him and praise his name" (Psalm 100:4).*

*"He who sacrifices thank offerings honors me,
and he prepares the way so that
I may show him the salvation of God" (Psalm 50:23).*

How close heaven and earth are to each other! Even sin could not drive a permanent wedge between them. This earth serves as the courtyard of the heavenly sanctuary. The courtyard work that Jesus performed in His humanity as our High Priest was accomplished right here on earth.

Early each morning the earthly priests began their daily work in the courtyard of the sanctuary. They entered reverently, chanting or singing praises to God. This praise honored God and prepared the way for Him to work in the salvation of the people. (See Psalm 50:23)

My morning praise time does not take place in a sacred courtyard, attended by white-robed priests. My study is my chapel, and my garb is quite informal. Yet I too begin either with singing, reading, or reciting a psalm of praise. What riches the book of Psalms brings to my devotional life. Praise to God never needs to be repetitious when I have 150 psalms to choose from to read or sing! However, repetition in words when praising God is not always undesirable. The angels sing "Holy, holy, holy." What counts is that the heart be turned toward God in true hunger, longing, and adoration.

Not only the Psalms but many other portions of Scripture speak in powerful language the praises of the Most High. My goal is to discover as many praise portions of the Bible as possible and speak them aloud in prayer. As I speak the words inspired by the Holy Spirit, my soul is lifted up to sing with the angels.

I desire to make this beginning time of my day wholly God-centered. I spent many years seeking His presence mainly to ask favors. In humility I now seek to discipline my mind to think of God as the ruler of the universe. I recall His mighty power, His creative mind, His endless love, His abundant mercy.

The thoughts that begin my day often carry over to the end of the day. One night sleep seemed impossible for me. As I lay awake long past the time I am usually fast asleep, my mind was drawn to my morning prayer-time and the greatness of God. I remembered the many descriptions the Bible gives us of God and His attributes. I began to list them in my mind: Creator of heaven and earth, Redeemer,

Prince of peace, Savior, Judge, immortal, eternal, Healer, Lord, Counselor, wonderful, majestic, perfect, holy, awesome, lovely, glorious, merciful, gracious, righteous, faithful, wise, all-powerful. On and on the wonderful list grew, and my sleeplessness became a blessing.

One morning I tried to think of the greatest and most powerful human being in the world to compare God with. The best I could come up with was the president of the United States. I tried to imagine myself speaking with him. It dawned on me that there is scarcely a chance in the world that I would ever be allowed to speak with the president! I would never even be able to get through to him on the telephone.

Then I thought of the governor of my state. The same is true of him. I don't have the prestige to speak with such powerful men. Now, the mayor of my city might be interested enough in my individual vote that he would somehow sandwich me in between some of his important appointments if I were persistent. But I would definitely be an intrusion into his day.

Then I thought of God, the ruler of the universe. Not only does He allow me to approach Him every day, but He is delighted that I come to speak with Him. Instead of an irritation, it makes His day happier when I spend time with Him. Oh, how can I not praise and love a God like that? What a hardhearted and selfish person I would be to neglect or avoid spending time with Him.

I have noticed the trend of some Christians today to feel that praise to God should involve only high and holy things—that we should center in on God's attributes separate from ourselves. But praise to God is not complete until we involve our personal lives in praise, voicing

14

thanksgiving for God's personal blessings. Praise and thanksgiving are often worded together in scripture. I offer personal thanks for the blessing of sleep, of good health, of time, of the specific blessings that have come my way. Sometimes I compose a verse, psalm, or prayer to save for rereading.

One morning, hearing the mocking birds outside my window as I began my morning prayer-time, the thought came to me that I am only one small part of God's creation who praise Him. I jotted down this small psalm of praise:

MOCKINGBIRD PSALM

Every morning the mockingbirds
  express
  their joy at being alive.
  Their little breasts
  fill with the breath of life,
  their vocal cords swell
  and they trill again and again
  in varying accents
  and combinations of notes.
  Praise Him, Praise Him,
  again and again
  they proclaim.

Lord, in the morning
  I too come to You
  with praise.
  May my joy be
  as great,
  my song as thankful,

15

my heart as humble,
as the mockingbird.

How much more we need to cultivate the habit of praise and thankfulness. As I spend more time in praise prayer, I find that my heart turns more naturally to thankfulness and appreciation for familiar daily blessings: bright blossoms on the vine outside my kitchen window, my light and airy house, my husband's smile, letters from my children.

I envy those for whom song bursts forth spontaneously and beautifully like the songbirds. But although I have not been endowed with a great gift of music, yet I am able to join in the fellowship of singing with others in the family, in church and in small worship groups. And sometimes I sing alone—almost every morning in my prayer time—but I sing only for God. I like to think that God sends an angel to sing along with me so that my hymn of praise reaches Him in purity and beauty.

As I share how I pray I am not giving you a model to follow, but an illustration of how God is leading in my life through Sanctuary Prayer. I pray that as you read you will be touched by the Holy Spirit with a desire to further develop your own personal relationship with God through praise and prayer.

When I present this topic in my seminars I emphasize the many opportunities for each person to praise God using the gifts God has given them—not being limited by trying to follow someone else's formula for worship but praising God as they are led by the Holy Spirit.

One afternoon at a Prayer Summit a woman greeted me with excitement.

16

"Carrol," she exclaimed, "thank you for telling me it is all right to play the piano during my prayer time. Oh, what a blessing this is to me!" She went on to say that sitting at her piano and playing and singing praise songs during her private morning worship was changing her relationship with God.

Although I remembered speaking with her briefly after a seminar several weeks before I recalled nothing specific from our conversation. Surely I had no memory of telling her (or anyone else) that piano playing was acceptable during prayer time. After all, who am I to tell anyone what they can or cannot do during personal prayer?

But I was delighted to hear of her creative way to worship God. Why not play your praises to God? On the piano, harp, guitar, organ, or harmonica? It's the worshiping heart that God sees and hears.

Somehow what I had said to her had awakened in this woman the desire to use her musical abilities to praise God. And she was blessed. That is what I desire for everyone as they praise God in prayer.

A favorite author of mine says, "Every individual has a life distinct from all others, and an experience differing essentially from theirs. God desires that our praise shall ascend to Him, marked by our own individuality."[1]

I hope that you, too, will persevere in a relationship with God in prayer until you find such joy in the Lord that your prayer time becomes your greatest pleasure. By then you will discover that your morning devotions do not end as you arise from prayer; you and God will continue your conversation as you go on with your day, and it can truly be said of you that you pray without ceasing.

17

MORNING PSALM

Praise the Lord!
Praise Him in morning worship;
    praise Him as the sun arises.
Praise Him for His providence;
    praise Him for His kindness
        and His mercy.
Praise Him with the voice of prayer;
    praise Him with repentance
        and confession.
Praise Him with faith and adoration;
    praise Him with openness
        and honesty.
Praise Him with words and with actions.
Let all whose hearts respond to God's grace
    praise the Lord.
        Praise the Lord!

SUMMARY

The first step in sanctuary prayer is to enter His courts with praise. I praise God for who He is: Creator, King of the universe, Savior, immortal, all-wise, etc.

I begin my prayer time by reading praise portions of Scripture, such as many of the psalms, chapters in Isaiah, Revelation, and other books of the Bible.

Some of my favorites are: Exodus 15:11; 1 Chronicles 29:10-13; Psalm 150; Psalm 47; Psalm 63:1-8; Psalm 84; Psalm 89:5-8; Psalm 93; Psalm 100; Isaiah 9:6, 7; Isaiah 12; Isaiah 40:12-31; Romans 11:33-36; Revelation 4:8, 11 (last part); Revelation 5:12, 13 (last parts of each verse);

Revelation 7:12; Revelation 15:3, 4; Of course, there are many, many more beautiful praise portions of the Bible. Have fun searching them out!

Praise to God is not complete until we involve our personal lives in praise, voicing thanksgiving for God's personal blessings. I add my appreciation for God's special gifts to me, my thankfulness for His constant care.

Use music whenever possible in your prayer time. What better way to praise God? Sometimes I sing a song of praise or write a bit of verse in my spiritual notebook. Music and poetry seem to be the language of praise. Personal prayer is a time to be wholly open to the Spirit's guidance. Let Him guide you in praise.

---

[1] E.G. White, *Desire of Ages*, page 347.

CHAPTER THREE

The Altar
of Sacrifice

"This is love: not that we loved God, but that he loved us
and sent his Son as an atoning sacrifice for our sins.
Dear friends, since God so loved us,
we also ought to love one another.
No one has ever seen God; but if we love one another,
God lives in us and his love is made complete in us."
(1 John 4:10-12)

In the sanctuary in the wilderness, as the priest entered the courtyard, the first item of furniture he came to was the bronze altar on which the animal sacrifice was slain and burned as a sin offering. That, of course, was only the earthly illustration. The real sacrifice for all sin was accomplished at the cross of Calvary.

As I come in my morning prayer-time to the altar of sacrifice, I bow low before the mighty Gift of God on the cross. I envision Jesus as He hung there for my sins.

"Lord," I cry, "forgive my sins." I remind Him of the promise: "If we confess our sins, he is faithful and just and will forgive us our sins and purify us from all unrighteousness" (1 John 1:9).

Just as the Israelite in the wilderness tabernacle trusted the priest to carry through the ritual of sacrifice that provided salvation, so I trust wholly in Jesus, my High Priest, for His mediation.

Many of us have grown up in a Christian home and came to know God as our Savior from sin in a gradual way. Yet some of us have found God in a sudden life-changing experience. We remember the lifting of the crushing burden of sin and the joy of forgiveness. We remember the sunshine that followed that experience.

What God is asking us to do here at the altar of sacrifice is to daily relive that experience of forgiveness. As we do this, we'll discover a depth of relationship with God that increases daily.

There is no blanket forgiveness for sin. Confession must be specific. Although in my evening prayer I confess any known sin, yet in the morning the Lord often impresses me with specific thoughts, actions, or words of mine that were unlike Christ that had not come to my mind the night before. The Lord is very gracious. He knows exactly the right time to speak to us about each sin. As I confess my specific sins and eagerly accept God's forgiveness, I give voice also to my great desire to be wholly His in every aspect of my life.

"Oh, Lord," I cry, "my greatest desire is to be one with You. Underlying all other, perhaps conflicting human desires, is my desire for You. Accept me as a living sacrifice. May I die to self and sin and live only for You."

It is here that I also discuss with God my sinful tendencies, the sins that so frequently overtake me. How can I ever overcome selfishness, impatience, daydreaming, worrying, depression, pride, fear? Do not think that talking these over with Jesus and the Father and the Holy Spirit is useless. In the past I often felt so hopeless about my weaknesses that I failed to talk them over with God. After all, they were my problems, not His. Besides, I was always sure that if I just tried harder I could overcome. But it never worked.

"'Come now, let us reason together,' says the Lord. 'Though your sins are like scarlet, they shall be as white as snow; though they are red as crimson, they shall be like wool'" (Isaiah 1:18).

As I began discussing my weaknesses with God in Sanctuary Prayer, I began to find victory. God has the answer to every thing I am willing to be open and honest about. The answer may not come immediately, but as I talk with Him, He is able to lead me to see root causes for sin, to recognize how one self-indulgence leads to the cropping out of what may even seem unrelated sins. He leads me step by step to a greater realization of my need and His power.

You see, true prayer is inspired by the Holy Spirit. That means that as I pray, the desires of my heart for oneness with God, for forgiveness, for victory over sin, are all impressed upon me by the Holy Spirit. These desires do not come from my natural human heart but from the heart of God. I am not only praying *to* God but *by* the power of God.

So as I pour out my heart's need for purity, for cleansing, for victory, I am praying God's desire for me. I can know He will answer my prayer. What a faith experience this kind of praying is!

It is here at the altar of sacrifice that I also pray through any darkness or disinterest that may plague my prayer time. If, as I come to God in the morning, I sense a shadow between myself and Him—a lack of love or desire for Him, or any feelings of resistance or doubt—I confess these openly and ask the Lord to show me any cherished sin that could be causing this response in me. "Take all of me," I pray. "1 freely give You my entire will, and what I am unable to give, I ask You to take. I choose You and only You to be the center of my life."

If the darkness persists, I ask God in the name of Jesus to rebuke Satan for casting his shadow across my path. I then once more confess my great need and desire to be wholly the Lord's in every part of my life.

Darkness pressing around us does not mean that God has forsaken us. Satan throws his shadows around us whenever he can. It is important that we realize the reality of the enemy. In the last chapter I spoke of God as the King of the universe and of His special delight in each individual. We are told that the relationship between God and each person is as close as though only those two exist in the universe. The counterpart of this is also true. There is an enemy who considers each one of us important to his ends.

I have few enemies on this earth. I know that there are many evil forces in world governments and evil people

23

who walk the earth. But somehow I cannot feel that I am important enough to be the target of an enemy. This thought carries over into the spiritual world, too. I know the devil is my enemy, but surely I am not important enough that he would actually center his attacks upon me.

But I have found that the devil who "prowls around like a roaring lion looking for someone to devour" (1 Peter 5:8) is just as interested in you and me as is God, though for very different reasons. Satan will go to any length to cause us suffering, discomfort, and even death. As Christians we need not fear, for we are well armored in the power of the Lord. But we do need to be aware that the devil and his personal attacks are real.

The Bible outlines exactly how to drive away this darkness from your prayer life:

"Submit yourselves, then, to God. Resist the devil, and he will flee from you. Come near to God and he will come near to you. Wash your hands, you sinners, and purify your hearts, you double-minded. Grieve, mourn and wail. Change your laughter to mourning and your joy to gloom. Humble yourselves before the Lord, and he will lift you up" (James 4:7-10).

Submission to God is the first step. We are to be in earnest about this. Our relationship with God must be the most important aspect of our life. We need to feel sincere grief for our sins. Paul tells us in Hebrew 12:2,3: "Let us fix our eyes on Jesus, the author and perfecter of our faith, who for the joy set before him endured the cross, scorning its shame, and sat down at the right hand of the throne of God. Consider him who endured such opposition from sinful men, so that you will not grow weary and lose heart."

24

Always look to Jesus. He took the full weight of the sins of humanity throughout earth time upon Himself in the Garden of Gethsemane and carried them to the cross. We need carry no such weight—not even the weight of our own sins if we have given them to Jesus. But we must realize the seriousness of sin. James says to "grieve, mourn, and wail." How many of us take our sins that seriously?

These verses do not mean that we as Christians must go around in mourning. No, Christians should be the most joyous people on earth. What James is telling us is that because human beings have no power to resist the devil on their own, we must first submit ourselves to God, who alone can help us see the enormity of our sins and give us the gift of repentance. Then we will "grieve, mourn, and wail." It's true that we are not as demonstrative in our emotions here in the western world as were the Jews of James' day. But we must have deep sorrow for our sins, a sorrow so deep that when we find forgiveness we will not willingly fall back into sin.

Also, remember that weeping endures only for a night. Joy comes in the morning (Psalm 30:5). When God gives us the power to resist the devil and makes Satan flee from us, our lives will be filled with joy.

When we have taken these steps to humble ourselves before the Lord, confessing our sinfulness, our weakness, and our desire for Him, and we resist Satan, then God will lift us up to worship with Him. Our grief will turn into joy.

God always allows us the power of choice. Every day we have opportunities to make choices that show our resolution to resist the tempter and keep our eyes on Jesus.

I have found that many of the authors of scripture had times when God seemed far away or there seemed to be a shadow between themselves and God. As I began searching out these passages, hoping to learn more of God's principles for overcoming darkness in my spiritual life, I discovered that even in their greatest discouragement these men would deliberately reach out to God, yearning for His felt presence.

I began using the words of these Bible writers in my own prayers. What a joy this has brought to my devotional times! I make the longing for God in these scripture passages my own yearning for God.

I have made a collection of my favorite 'Yearning' verses.[1] One passage which is especially meaningful to me is Psalm 63:1-8. As you read these verses it will give you an idea of what to look for as you search for verses that express your own longing for God:

> "O God, you are my God,
>   earnestly I seek you;
> my soul thirsts for you,
>   my body longs for you,
> in a dry and weary land
>   where there is no water.
>
> "I have seen you in the sanctuary
>   and beheld your power and your glory.
> Because your love is better than life,
>   my lips will glorify you.

I will praise you as long as I live,
    and in your name I will lift up my hands.

"My soul will be satisfied as
    with the richest of foods;
with singing lips my mouth will praise you.

"On my bed I remember you;
    I think of you through the watches of the night.
Because you are my help,
    I sing in the shadow of your wings.
My soul clings to you;
    your right hand upholds me."

For most Christians today disinterest in prayer is usually caused by allowing the cares of this life to keep us from Bible study and prayer. This in turn makes God seem far away and prayer almost drudgery. This becomes a vicious circle even to those who honestly love God. But I believe that deliberately setting aside time each day for Bible study and prayer and praying verses of longing will cut through the veneer of care and pain and soften almost any heart and lead them directly into heartfelt prayer.

Reading Scripture is a great mind up-lifter at all times and a valuable asset in prayer. A friend shared with me a simple tool used in therapy to combat panic attacks: breathe in deeply through the nostrils, breathe out through the mouth. She likened this to the antidote for spiritual panic attacks: *Breathe in the promises of God, breathe out praises.* (I like that!)

I love the promises of God. They lead me to thank God for His continual faithfulness. Here are some of my morning favorites:

"Here is a trustworthy saying: If we died with him we will also live with him; if we endure, we will also reign with him. If we disown him, he will also disown us; if we are faithless, he will remain faithful, for he cannot disown himself" (2 Timothy 2:11-13).

"Here is a trustworthy saying that deserves full acceptance: Christ Jesus came into the world to save sinners — of whom I am the worst" (1 Timothy. 1:15).

(How I love these "trustworthy" passages! The apostle Paul had such a unique way of emphasizing truths! We know that all scripture is trustworthy—but when Paul wanted to show that something was especially important he would announce to everyone that *this passage is trustworthy*.)

"I have been crucified with Christ and I no longer live, but Christ lives in me. The life I live in the body, I live by faith in the Son of God, who loved me and gave Himself for me" (Galatians 2:20). (How His love warms my heart!)

"Since, then, you have been raised with Christ, set your hearts on things above, where Christ is seated at the right hand of God. Set your minds on things above, not on earthly things. For you died, and your life is now hidden with Christ in God" (Colossians 3:1-3). (Hide me, O Lord, with You.)

The Lord is faithful. He is able, and He does pierce the darkness and light up my life. I believe that the key to rising above the darkness is to reach out to God in intensity of desire, just as Jacob put forth his greatest strength in struggling with the angel.

A religious writer of another century wrote:

"Jacob prevailed because he was persevering and determined. His victory is an evidence of the power of importunate prayer. All who will lay hold of God's promises, as he did, and be as earnest and persevering as he was will succeed as he succeeded. Those who are unwilling to deny self, to agonize before God, to pray long and earnestly for His blessing, will not obtain it. Wrestling with God—how few know what it is! How few have ever had their souls drawn out after God with intensity of desire until every power is on the stretch. When waves of despair which no language can express sweep over the suppliant, how few cling with unyielding faith to the promises of God."[2]

"When thick clouds of darkness seem to hover over the mind, then is the time to let living faith pierce the darkness and scatter the clouds. True faith rests on the promises contained in the Word of God, and those only who obey that Word can claim its glorious promises."[3]

Have you wondered how to agonize with God—or why agonizing with God is even necessary? Why would God desire it? This agony is exemplified in the bronze altar experience of Sanctuary Prayer. We need to open our hearts and lives wholly to God, letting Him bring out of the *depths of our hearts our desire for Him* and be *willing to give up every cherished practice or thought that separates us from Him.* (Biblical examples: Jacob as he wrestled with the angel; Christ in Gethsemane.)

The sacrifice most often offered on the altar in the earthly sanctuary was a lamb, representing Jesus. God once gave me an illustration of that sacrifice, which took me several years to understand. But once understood, I can never forget it, for it touches my heart so deeply.

Several years ago my husband surprised me with the gift of fluffy white lambskin seat covers for my little red Buick Skylark. The contrast of the white seat covers with the maroon interior and the red exterior of my car pleased me.

A few days after we had installed them, my 4-year-old granddaughter Kimi went for a ride with me. Kimi likes new things—and pretty things—so after I had safely installed her in her car seat, she investigated my new seat covers. In silence she surveyed them, fingered them.

"Grandma," she asked, "did they have to cut a sheep to get your seat covers?"

I gulped. I hadn't thought of it in that light before. It doesn't hurt a lamb to remove its wool, but lambskin cannot be removed from a live lamb. In order for me to have lambskin seat covers for my car, a lamb had to die.

"Well, yes, Kimi," I finally managed to say. "Yes, I guess that someone did have to cut a lamb to make these seat covers."

She sat in silence, looking straight ahead as I started the car. "Grandma," she finally said, looking at me sadly, maybe sternly, "I don't think God likes you to cut sheep to make seat covers."

Suddenly I didn't like my new seat covers anymore. They didn't wear well, either, and I was glad when I finally could replace them with man-made fleece covers.

That was years ago. Kimi is now grown-up. But God taught me a lesson from that story. Here is how it happened: I was listening to a tape. The speaker began to pray. In his prayer he thanked the Lord for dying and for giving us His fleece. I had never heard anyone word a prayer just like that. In my mind's eye my lambskin seat covers appeared, and I saw that they represented the fleece of the Lamb of God. Unless a knife was applied to the Lamb, I could not be covered by His fleece. His death made my covering possible.

"Yes," I silently said to the long-ago 4-year-old, "1 see it now. They did have to cut a Lamb to make a covering for you and me."

In my imagination I was back in Eden. The first sinners had just discovered that they were naked. An innocent Eden animal was brought forward, killed, and from its skin God Himself fashioned garments for Adam and Eve. They could never forget that an animal had to be cut so that they could be clothed.

Jesus Himself was the Lamb slain for my sins, the Lamb without spot or blemish. His beautiful fleece, His perfect righteousness, was made into a covering for you and me.

SUMMARY

The second step in sanctuary prayer is at the altar of sacrifice, which represents the sacrifice of Jesus on the cross.

I come to the cross with a humble and contrite heart. I confess any specific sin that I am conscious of, asking God to reveal to me anything that separates me from Him. I also confess my sinfulness and weakness and discuss with God my besetting sins—the sins I fall into so easily (James 4:7-10). I tell Him that it is my deepest desire to please Him in all things. I repent of carelessness of the past and

31

give over to God the specific areas of my life in which I have been negligent.

I claim Bible promises for forgiveness. (1 John 1:9; Galatians 2:20; Romans 12:1, 2.) I tell God that it is my desire to be a living sacrifice and to live today wholly for Him. I press through any discouragement or disinterest that may darken my prayer time.

In James 4:7-10 God has given us a formula for pressing through the darkness: "Submit yourselves, then, to God. Resist the devil, and he will flee from you. Come near to God and he will come near to you. Wash your hands, you sinners, and purify your hearts, you double-minded. Grieve, mourn and wail. Change your laughter to mourning and your joy to gloom. Humble yourselves before the Lord, and he will lift you up."

Intensity of desire, such as Jacob had as he fought the angel at the River Jabbok, is the key to driving away the darkness. This is called 'agonizing' in prayer, and is a necessary tool for survival in the end-time.

I fill my mind with promises of God's greatness and power and the wonderful things He desires to do for me. This builds my faith and increases my joy. Because of Christ's death on the cross, represented by the Altar of Sacrifice in the wilderness sanctuary, I can know my sins are forgiven.

---

[1] To order a set of 18 Yearning Verses in attractive card form, email the author at *cjshewmake@prayerpartners.com* for price information.
[2] E.G. White, *The Great Controversy*, p. 621.
[3] White, *Early Writings*, pp. 72, 73

CHAPTER FOUR

The Laver
of Washing

*"Cleanse me with hyssop, and I will be clean;
wash me, and I will be whiter than snow."
(Psalm 51:7)*

Water! What an important part it plays in our physical lives. We drink it, bathe in it, play in it. Its therapeutic value is well-known. Our planet would be a barren desert without water. Abundant water changes the desert to a garden of delight.

Just beyond the altar of sacrifice in the courtyard of the Mosaic sanctuary was a bronze basin called the laver. It provided water for washing the feet and hands of the priest before he entered to minister in the Holy Place or to offer a burnt offering.

As I come before God in the morning, confessing my sins at the bronze altar of sacrifice, Jesus forgives me and washes away my sin with His blood. But now at the laver He asks me to step further into His plan. I don't know myself, but God knows that daily contact with the world often contaminates me and dims my desire for the Lord. (This is not necessarily so. Christians must ever live in the world but need not be infected by the world. However, we often find ourselves in Lot's shoes, moving closer and closer to the world.) But God has a remedy for every human predicament.

At the laver His plan for us is that we step still deeper into His will. He calls for us to be baptized. If we have already made the necessary public witness of baptism, all He asks of us each day is to make the same decision to follow Him over again with the same earnestness. He asks us to rededicate our lives to Him.

Jesus, when He came to earth as a human being, took the step of baptism as our example. The Bible tells us that in preparation for His public ministry He came to the river Jordan to be baptized of His cousin, John the Baptist. Luke records this experience: "When all the people were being baptized, Jesus was baptized too. And as he was praying, heaven was opened and the Holy Spirit descended on him in bodily form like a dove. And a voice came from heaven: 'You are my Son, whom I love; with you I am well pleased.'"(Luke 3:21, 22).

We do not often hear the audible voice of God today. But when we daily rededicate our lives to Him at the laver, by faith the Father is saying to us--yes, to you and to me— "I love you. You are my child and I'm pleased with you."

The apostle Paul, speaking of the relationship of husbands and wives, compared it to the relationship of Christ and the church. He said that Christ so loved the church that He gave Himself that the church might become holy. Paul goes on to say that Christ cleanses the church through washing with water through the Word (see Ephesians 5:25-27). The Word of God has cleansing properties. I need to be washed in the Word daily, just as I need to bathe daily for my physical health. There is no other way to remain clean than to be often in the Word. If I spend more time in secular entertainment and reading, or watching television, even good programs, than I do in reading the Bible and meditating on the Word, I cannot grow in Christ.

In the story of the vine and the branches, Jesus gave His disciples an illustration of their total dependence upon God. He spoke of the trimming done by the Father to prepare the branches to bear fruit. Then He said, "You are already clean because of the word I have spoken to you" (John 15:3). Cleansed by words of Jesus! Can I expect today that His words will clean me?

Jesus in his last prayer for His twelve disciples and for those who would accept the gospel throughout earth history, asked the Father to preserve the purity of His special people. He said, "My prayer is not that you take them out of the world but that you protect them from the evil one. They are not of the world, even as I am not of it. Sanctify them by the truth; your word is truth" (John 17:15-17). The emphasis for both cleansing and keeping is upon the Word.

After you have worked with certain chemicals, prepared fruit or vegetables to can or freeze, worked in the garden or repaired the car, if you have not worn gloves, every crease and line on your hands is outlined in color. Often the stain does not come off if you wash with water only. It takes a special soap to get your hands really clean again. Sometimes sin has the same effect upon us. We are forgiven, but a residue of past sinning stains the creases of our minds.

My heart sometimes almost breaks with longing to be pure and holy before Him, to come into His presence in innocence. But we can never wear the white robes of innocence that Adam and Eve wore in the Garden of Eden. Adam and Eve lost those when they ate of the tree of knowledge of good and evil. And because they lost them, not one of their descendants can wear them either. First hand knowledge of sin is our inheritance.

"Who may ascend the hill of the Lord? Who may stand in his holy place? He who has clean hands and a pure heart, who does not lift up his soul to an idol or swear by what is false" (Psalm 24:3, 4).

Psalm 24 has long been one of my favorite passages. Yet the reference to "clean hands" and a "pure heart" has always caused me concern. How, I wondered, could it ever be possible? The sanctuary gives me the answer. As I come to the laver each morning, God washes away sin, cleansing deeper and deeper as I continue to rededicate my life to Him.

No ordinary water can wash away the contamination of sin. Only the water of life—living water—which flows from the pierced side of Jesus can do that. He will rebaptize me daily in the laver and clothe me in a beautiful white robe—the lovely garment of Christ's perfect righteousness, worked out in His perfect human life. Jesus is able to give me His sinless life because He bore my sins upon the cross. The price for sin has been paid.

David wrote the fifty-first psalm in contrition of heart after his great public and private sin: "Cleanse me with hyssop, and I will be clean; wash me, and I will be whiter than snow" (Psalm 51:7).

Now, I don't know much about hyssop except that it is a plant of some sort. How it was used for cleaning I do not know. But I'm an expert at using scrub brushes, soap, and cleansing powder. So when I feel overwhelmed at my uncleanness, I ask the Lord to scrub me inside and out with the strongest cleaning agents possible.

"Use a bottle brush, Lord," I pray, "so You can reach every spot and crevice of my heart and mind where the soil of sin may remain. Scrub me clean!"

The laver always reminds me of foot washing. It's natural that it should, I suppose, for that was its original use—the washing of the feet and hands of the priests. But the foot washing that touches my heart is the story of Jesus and His disciples in the upper room that last night as they ate the Passover lamb. Jesus was the only one of the group who realized that it was the last supper He would eat with His disciples. He was sorrowful—for Himself, but more for His disciples who did not comprehend the extent of His mission.

I have experienced enough sorrow in my life to have a vague appreciation of how Jesus felt that night as He faced the hardest experience of His life. Yet His first thoughts were for His confused disciples, still arguing who was to be greatest in the earthly kingdom they believed He was soon to set up.

The Bible account says that Jesus took a basin—a laver—and a towel and began to wash their feet. When

37

Peter objected because of his pride, Jesus said, "Unless I wash you, you have no part with me" (John 13:8).

I remember another foot washing that touched my heart too. My husband was pastoring a church in a beach city that teemed with homeless young people during the late 1960's hippie era. God had placed a burden for those wanderers upon several students at the nearby Christian college. Thus began a thrilling time for my husband and me as we participated with the college students in a program to reach out with the gospel to those homeless young people.

Word got around among the hippie young people that they would be welcomed at our church and would be given a meal following the service. Our traditional church members (and that included me) were really tested to accept the crowds that descended upon us. We suspected, perhaps rightly, that the young people came solely for the food. I remember several Sabbaths when ten to twenty beach people came in after the church service had begun. They sat on the floor even though there were seats available. We felt uncomfortable.

Then came the Sabbath when the communion service was scheduled. I was determined to enjoy the service despite the presence of these unusual young people. I did my best to set aside my uneasiness and concentrate on Jesus. Beside me sat a young couple, their long hair, and wan faces contrasting with the well-fed look of our congregation. My husband explained simply but beautifully why our church practices the ordinance of humility, how by washing one another's feet, we exemplify Christ and have the opportunity to not only rededicate our lives to him, but also to reach out to each other with God's love.

When the men and women separated to other rooms for the service of humility, I lost sight of the young couple. I looked around for the girl in the fellowship hall where the women had retired, but didn't see her. I dismissed her from my mind.

But later as I sat quietly in the church, waiting while the congregation reassembled to drink the wine and eat the bread, the boy and girl slipped back into their seats beside me.

I couldn't help overhearing the girl ask, "Ed, did you take part?"

"Well, I went in to where the men were, but no one paid any attention to me. So I just filled a basin with water and took a towel and washed my own feet."

Strange feelings stirred me as I heard Ed's reply—but the girl was indignant!

"Ed, what a thing to do! It's to make you humble that you wash someone else's feet. How could washing your own feet do any good?"

I darted a quick sidewise look at Ed. He was the picture of dejection, his long hair falling over half his downcast face. Just then he looked up, a smile of singular sweetness lighting his countenance.

"Well—you see, God knows my heart!"

Quietness reigned in our row. The organ music swelled in sweet majesty.

"Ed," the girl spoke again. "Ed, I take it back. It was more humbling to wash your own feet."

As I partook of the bread and wine side by side with the young couple, I heard my husband's voice as he spoke of Christ's blood and body. I heard my husband's voice, but I saw Christ and His twelve friends, with their flowing robes and their dusty feet. I saw Jesus tenderly wash their feet and then serve them wine and bread. I saw this and marveled as I realized that God really does know our hearts.

"O Lord," I pray again today as I write this, "take away my traditional fears and expectations. Make me open to Your voice and open to the needs around me. Make me honest. Help me to see Your searching children no matter what clothes they wear or whatever their living styles. Forgive my bigotry and pride. Wash me clean."

The laver was made from the brass mirrors given to the Israelite women by the Egyptians as farewell gifts. The women gave up pride in their appearance and donated the mirrors to God for the building of the sanctuary. It is very meaningful to me that it was the basin of washing that was melded from the mirrors.

Pride is one of my worst enemies. Not only vanity, but pride in a hundred different forms. Every day I must relinquish my pride in the specific areas God reveals to me.

One of the activities I have found most meaningful at the laver is what I call an exchange plan. I ask the Lord to exchange:

- my vacillating will for His unfaltering obedience
- my world-filled mind for the heaven-filled mind of Jesus
- my pride for His humble submission
- my fear for His perfect love
- my weakness for His strength

Now, this exchange does not come about by magic. God does not deal in magic. But He does deal in miracles. The greatest miracle of all is a regenerated heart, and that He has already given me. The rest of the exchange He works out just as fast as I am ready to cooperate with Him in His instruction and discipline. When I most need His attributes I find that they are mine. He is ever faithful.

SUMMARY

The third step of sanctuary prayer is at the laver of washing. I come to the laver each morning, freshly forgiven at the cross and desiring to have the residue of sin washed out of my heart and life. It has two purposes for me, to wash me clean and to renew my devotion to God. I like to think of the laver as a baptistery where I daily rededicate my life to God. Daily I am able to hear the inward voice of the Holy Spirit saying, "You are my beloved child in whom I am well pleased."

The Bible speaks of three things that cleanse us: the blood of the Lamb of God, the water of baptism, and the Word of God. I come each morning seeking a new baptism. I ask for clean hands and a pure heart, that both my actions and my thoughts and motives may please God.

Like David in Psalm 51:7, I ask God to scrub me clean: "Cleanse me with hyssop, and I will be clean; wash me, and I will be whiter than snow."

Daily I need to be washed in the word of God. I keep my Bible handy as I pray, and whenever the Holy Spirit brings a text to my mind, I look it up and read it. Truth is the only thing that will wipe the world from my heart.

I have an exchange plan that I use at the laver. I ask God to exchange my weakness for His strength, my selfishness for His love, my pride for His humble submission, my sinfulness for His perfect righteousness.

Praise God for the lessons of the laver!

CHAPTER FIVE

The Lampstand
of the Holy Spirit

"If you then, though you are evil,
know how to give good gifts to your children,
how much more will your Father in heaven
give the Holy Spirit to those who ask him!"
(Luke 11:13)

The seven-branched lampstand in the earthly sanctuary, fed by holy oil, lit up the entire sanctuary with a light that was never allowed to go out. God was very particular in His instructions as to the care and maintenance of this light, for it represented the eternal vigilance of the Holy Spirit.

Although I learn about God from the earthly illustration, the reality is in heaven. Faith allows me morning by morning to enter heaven's holy places where God dwells. When I come to the lampstand as I follow the steps of Sanctuary Prayer, I have already begun my prayer time with praise to our magnificent God as I entered by faith the courtyard of heaven. I have received forgiveness at the altar of sacrifice (representing the cross of Calvary where Jesus died the eternal death for sinners). I have been washed clean at the laver of washing (representing the cleansing of the Word of God and rebaptism), and now I come to the lampstand, where the oil of the Holy Spirit lights up the Holy Place.

When I first began praying through the sanctuary and realized that I was by faith entering the heavenly sanctuary, I made a startling discovery at the lampstand. From reading the Bible I knew that the light from the lampstand, which was never allowed to go out was fueled by oil made from ingredients especially chosen by God and blended by the priests. This light represented the eternal presence of the Holy Spirit. But what surprised me was the *personal* element I soon discovered at the lampstand.

I was reading one morning in Revelation, chapter 1, the story told by the apostle John of the vision he had of Christ among the seven lampstands (verses 9-20). I was struck by the lampstands in this story. Could they have a connection with the seven-branched lampstand in the sanctuary? Obviously, yes, they were related to the sanctuary. Sanctuary illustrations are throughout the book of Revelation. Although John's vision has a larger meaning especially for the church of God, yet I was amazed at the *personal* application I found.

In the Revelation story Jesus told John that the seven lampstands represented seven churches. Whenever God talks about a church He is talking about the people who make up the church. That's you and me. I remembered

Paul's reference to our bodies being the temple of God (1 Corinthians 3:16, 17; 5:21, 22) and grasped a new truth: *We are all lampstands for the Holy Spirit.* The oil represents the Holy Spirit but *we* are chosen containers to hold the Holy Spirit. I was amazed at how God's prophecies and counsel about nations, churches, and groups, can also be distilled to touch us individually and personally.

Every person receives the Holy Spirit at the time he or she is born-again into the Kingdom of God (Ephesians 1:13, 14; 2 Corinthians 1:21, 22). But if you read these verses carefully, you will notice that the amount first given is called a "deposit guaranteeing what is to come." Evidently God is enabled to give more and more of the Holy Spirit as the new Christian matures in his Christian life of service. We cannot rest upon what we received when we first came to the Lord. God wants to give us more!

How do we receive the fullness of the Holy Spirit? By asking for it.

Jesus counseled His disciples: "Which of you fathers, if your son asks for a fish, will give him a snake instead? Or if he asks for an egg, will give him a scorpion? If you then, though you are evil, know how to give good gifts to your children, *how much more will your Father in heaven give the Holy Spirit to those who ask him!*" (Luke 11:11-13, italics mine).

As we come daily before our Father, asking for the Holy Spirit to guide us in our walk with Him throughout the day, the amount we receive is determined by how empty we are of self and sin.

Review in your mind the first three steps of Sanctuary Prayer:

45

1) We enter the courtyard praising God for His Omniscient powers, for His salvation for us individually, and thanking Him for His personal blessings to us.

2) Next the sanctuary leads us through the experience of emptying our hearts and lives of sin by confessing and repenting at the altar of sacrifice (symbolizing the cross).

3) We yield ourselves to being washed clean at the laver (rebaptism).

These are the steps the sanctuary shows us to take *before* we come to ask for the Holy Spirit. How wonderful is God's sanctuary illustration, preparing our hearts to receive the fullness of the Holy Spirit daily!

When I first began sanctuary prayer, I was a bit cautious in approaching the lampstand. It had always been my habit to ask the Holy Spirit each morning to give me wisdom (James 1:5) and wise words to speak (Proverbs 22:17, 18). Daily I trusted God to do those things for me. But when I began sanctuary praying, it became obvious that asking for the infilling of the Holy Spirit at the lampstand involved a total dedication, an experience that was new to me.

I am naturally beset by fears. The thought of being filled with the fullness of God was frightening. Perhaps God might ask me to do something that I didn't feel qualified to do, or was too frightened to do—or just didn't want to do!

I have found that my commitment at the lampstand has to be a matter of trust. My greatest desire is to be wholly the Lord's. On that basic premise I gradually came to trust Him more completely to direct my life, not only as He sees fit but also as I would desire if I could see the end from the beginning.

E. G. White says, "God never leads His children otherwise than they would choose to be led, if they could see the end from the beginning, and discern the glory of the purpose which they are fullfilling as co-workers with Him."[1]

You see, God never asks us to do anything He does not prepare us to do. Remember God's preparation time for Moses? Eighty years! Not because it took God that long, but because it took that long for Moses to submit his will entirely. But God waited patiently until Moses was ready. How thankful we can be for God's patience with each of us. I trust that as I continue to grow in the Lord I will also grow more stable and mature.

God's personal desire for each of us is that we receive the fullness of the Spirit daily. We do not recognize the numerous losses we have experienced because of our failure to ask for the Holy Spirit. How different would be our relationship with God today if we had received the Holy Spirit in the past as He was available.

As I come daily to the lampstand, I determine not to let the unfilled past haunt me, but to receive today what the Holy Spirit has for me. An amazing attribute of God is His ability to redeem the past. "1 will repay you," He told Israel, "for the years the locust have eaten" (Joel 2:25). Remember the story Jesus told of the laborers hired at different times of the day? They all received the same pay. As humans we object to this pay scale, claiming "Unfair" because the time worked was unequal. The older brother of the prodigal son felt the same way about time. But with God, time is irrelevant.

"With the Lord a day is like a thousand years, and a thousand years are like a day" (2 Peter 3:8).

47

It is not that God does not care about time. He cares greatly. We are told that our time is a talent not to be squandered. We should repent of not having asked for the Holy Spirit in the past. But having repented, we should go on to utilize today's opportunities. God is able to use us today, even if it is our last day on earth. Also, even if it is the only day we ever served Him, He can help us do an incredible work with eternal consequences.

One morning God showed me how different His view of time was from mine. I had discovered *The Screwtape Letters,* by C. S. Lewis, and was delighted with it. Lewis talked about the troughs of dryness and depression, when Christianity seems less than real to the Christian. At such times the Christian often feels that he is estranged from God, but in reality it is at those times that he grows the most spiritually. He must then follow God strictly from faith, for his sight or feelings reveal nothing.

Well, I was very excited as I thought about that message. I could hardly wait to be depressed so that I could grow!

One morning I awoke depressed. As I gazed into the mirror I realized that here was my great opportunity to experiment with Lewis's conclusion. I became excited about the whole adventure. Then I realized that I was no longer depressed; nothing I thought of could renew my depression.

"Oh, dear," I said in disappointment, "I missed my opportunity to grow."

But God immediately impressed upon me a truth I have never forgotten. One doesn't need time to grow in God's way. Oh, it often takes us a long time to grow, but that is not necessary. God can mature a submitted heart in a very short period of time. Because I had seen a new dimension of God and had submitted to it, I had grown in just the way God desired me to grow, although it had taken only a fraction of a minute. Don't we serve a marvelous God?

As I come to the lampstand every morning, freshly emptied of sin and self at the altar of sacrifice and washed at the laver, I am ready to be filled with the fullness of God. This is an important and necessary step to take each day if I truly desire to be of service to God. Jesus told His disciples to wait in Jerusalem until they were endowed from on high with the Holy Spirit. The fullness the disciples received at Pentecost is available to us today. The Spirit cannot be used by human beings, but the Spirit longs to use us. The purpose of the infilling at the lampstand is always to enable us for service to God and mankind.

I love to study and learn of the Lord. I sometimes think that 1 could remain at the Iampstand and in the Most Holy Place learning forever and be happy with only His presence. But knowledge grows stale and dull if not shared. We keep fresh our experience with the Lord by sharing it with someone else. Then it can never die.

I try to find someone with whom I can share every insight or blessing received from the Lord the very day I receive it. If that doesn't seem appropriate I write it in my spiritual notebook because I have found that more likely than not I will forget a signal blessing from God if I do not write it down or tell someone else.

Perhaps you may wonder how you will know if your prayer for the infilling of the Holy Spirit worked, if you are in actuality filled with the Spirit after your prayer. Remember how at Creation God spoke, and "it was so"?

49

That is how you become Spirit-filled. God is faithful to His promises, and *it is so,* if you asked, believing. Just remember that God's promise is not for ecstasy but for peace.

WHAT CAN I EXPECT TO HAPPEN WHEN I RECEIVE THE HOLY SPIRIT?

As I accepted the fullness of the Spirit in my life I desired to know more about the Spirit and how I could expect Him to work in me. So I read a lot. A Bible concordance and a Bible gave me the needed tools for investigation. I found that the Holy Spirit works not only with Christians but also in the world. He convicts those who have never accepted Christ of their guilt of the sin of rejecting Him as their Redeemer. He also shows them the contrast between righteousness and sin (John 16:8-11).

There is a difference in how the Holy Spirit is able to work with those who have never invited Him into their hearts than with the born-again Christian. With the Christian the Holy Spirit works not only on the circumstances around the Christian, but He is able to work on the inside of the heart as that is His dwelling place. But with the unbeliever the Holy Spirit must work on the outside—through circumstances, trials, nature, and encounters with Christians—sometimes even with angels. Stories from third world countries where there are many towns and villages who have never heard the gospel give us amazing accounts. One such true story is that in one isolated village in the Philippines, a heathen chief heard the rocks around his village speak aloud about the true God. Who spoke through the rocks to introduce this ignorant heathen to God?

God is at work giving everyone an opportunity to choose to serve Him and obtain eternal life. The last work of the Holy Spirit to those who are lost will be to convince them that God was just and right, and that Satan was wrong. The lost will realize that they have followed the wrong leader; they had been willingly misled (again see John 16:8-11).

I was very interested in discovering the ways I could expect the Holy Spirit to involve Himself in my life so that I could cooperate with Him. Too often, it seems that I battle against what God is doing in my life.

So I looked in the Bible for stories of Spirit-filled people. I found interesting narratives of amazing things. But it was as I studied the life of Christ that I learned the most. Jesus was Spirit-filled from birth, of course, and in that way He differs from us. But we are promised the same power in our lives when we are born-again of the Spirit that He had throughout His life as a human being.

WHAT WAS THE ROLE OF THE HOLY SPIRIT IN THE LIFE OF JESUS?

Two passages in the book of Isaiah are prophecies of what God the Father and God the Holy Spirit would do for God the Son when He became a human being to enable Him to live a sinless life. In Isaiah 11:1-5 the prophet speaks of the Branch, which was a name given to the coming Messiah, and mentions the ways the Spirit would rest upon Him:

"The Spirit of the Lord will rest on him—the Spirit of wisdom and of understanding, the Spirit of counsel and of power, the Spirit of knowledge and of the fear of the Lord —and he will delight in the fear of the Lord. He will not judge by what he sees with his eyes, or decide by what he hears with his ears; but with righteousness he will judge the needy, with justice he will give decisions for the poor of the earth" (Isaiah 11:2-4, first part).

THE SEVEN ASPECTS OF THE
SEVEN-FOLD SPIRIT OF GOD

Let's list the attributes mentioned in this passage from Isaiah:

- Wisdom
- Understanding
- Counsel
- Power
- Knowledge
- Fear of the Lord
- Righteous judgment

In studying the life of Christ, we can see that He was surely blessed in all seven aspects of the Spirit's infilling mentioned in this text. Even as a child it was evident that He was "filled with wisdom" (Luke 2:40). When Jesus began His ministry, people were impressed by the authority with which He taught (Mark 1:22). What a contrast between the Spirit-filled Jesus and the Spirit-destitute teachers of the law! Everyone recognized the difference. Oh, there was no doubt that Jesus was not only filled with wisdom and power, but everything else that Isaiah had prophesied of Him—the complete, sevenfold Spirit.

One of the seven attributes of the Holy Spirit given to Jesus from His birth is mentioned twice in the Bible passage. Why is it mentioned twice? Did it have special significance in the life of Jesus? Isaiah says that not only was He filled with the 'fear of the Lord' but that He *delighted* in it. Evidently this was Jesus' favorite aspect of the Holy Spirit's infilling.

I found that the fear of the Lord is mentioned many times in the Bible, each time noting what the fear of the Lord will do in our lives—but never seeming to define what the fear of the Lord is. Here is a sample of what I found:

"The *fear of the Lord* is the beginning of wisdom" (Psalm111:10).

"The *fear of the Lord* is the beginning of knowledge (Proverbs 1:7).

"Through the *fear of the Lord* a man avoids evil" (Proverbs 16:6).

"The *fear of the Lord* adds length to life" (Proverbs 10:27).

"*The fear of the Lord* is a fountain of life" (Proverbs14:27).

"The *fear of the Lord* is pure" (Psalm 19:9).

"The *fear of the Lord* leads to life" (Proverbs 19:23).

"Humility and *the fear of the Lord* bring wealth and honor and life" (Proverbs 22:4).

"To *fear the Lord* is to hate evil" (Proverbs 8:13). (All italics mine.)

My conclusion is that the fear of the Lord is a basic ingredient for living a righteous life, *the foundation of spiritual infilling.* We see this aspect of the Spirit at work in the life of Jesus:

"During the days of Jesus' life on earth, he offered up prayers and petitions with loud cries and tears to the one who could save him from death, and he was heard because of his reverent submission" (Hebrews 5:7). The KJV in translating this verse, says that He "was heard in that he feared."   This gives us a clue as to what the fear of the Lord is: *The fear of the Lord is reverent submission to God.* How fitting that this was the part of serving His Father that Jesus most delighted in! Jesus often said that He did everything His Father asked Him to do.

"I desire to do your will, O my God; your law is within my heart" (Psalm 40:8).

"For I have come down from heaven not to do my will but to do the will of him who sent me" (John 6:38).

"The one who sent me is with me; he has not left me alone, for I always do what pleases him" (John 8:29). (How I long to be like Jesus!)

Another Old Testament prophecy from Isaiah further explains God's plans for the Spirit to work in the life of the human Jesus:

"The Sovereign Lord has given me
      an instructed tongue,
    to know the word that sustains the weary.
  He wakens me morning by morning,
      wakens my ear to listen like one being taught"
        (Isaiah 50:4).

This verse explains how Jesus could speak with authority, how He always knew the right words of encouragement and admonition for the people around Him, why He arose early in the morning to pray and often spent whole nights in prayer.

Will God do the same for us? Yes! What He did for Jesus He longs to do for us. These passages tell me that God will awaken me every morning to meet with Him and that He will fill me daily with His Spirit if I but ask. He will instruct me how to speak to the weary and needy if I answer His morning call to be taught by Him.

As I come to the lampstand daily I seek to cooperate intelligently with the Spirit's working in my life. And especially I ask for the fear of the Lord—reverent submission to God's will for me. And to make sure that I remember to do this I remind God of His promise to write His law in my heart (Hebrews 8:10).

The very next weekend after I received the above insight, the Lord gave me a practical illustration of how He desires this attribute of the Holy Spirit to work in my life. My husband, John, and I had spent a very busy but especially blessed Sabbath at our church. After vespers we came home hungry. Together we fixed a simple snack supper. John popped corn—he can't imagine Saturday night without popcorn—and I fixed a plate of fresh apple slices and slices of mild cheddar and jack cheeses. That, with a fruit drink, was a pleasant Saturday night supper. We sat down at the dining room table to eat our supper and play our favorite word game, Changeling.

Everything tasted so good—apple and cheese slices, together with popcorn. Soon I realized that I had eaten enough. It was time to stop eating. I looked at the plate of cheese slices remaining. It was obvious that I had sliced too much cheese for just the two of us. We hadn't eaten cheese for quite a while. I had, in fact, been cutting down on cheese, deciding that it was not the best food for us to eat. I had almost forgotten how good cheese tasted!

As I sat there musing I realized something else, too. Unless I got up and put the cheese away in the refrigerator I would most likely nibble on it until it was all gone.

55

I thought of how so many things in my life were like that. I often knew what I should do, but past experiences had programmed me to follow my human desires. I felt unbearably sad.

Where, oh, where, was the way to freedom? I knew that even if I put the cheese away now I would fail God another time in some other similar way. And there are many, many Christians just like me. This time I felt sorry for God.

"O Lord," I prayed, "how are You ever going to prepare a people for Your coming when we are all so weak?" Sadly I contemplated the slices of cheese.

"He delighted in the fear of the Lord." I recognized the voice of the Holy Spirit in my spiritual ear, quoting Scripture to answer my question, showing me how the human Jesus had superseded human desires in the freedom of the Spirit.

Excitedly I began to realize the importance of this revelation. Jesus had always delighted in reverent submission to His Father. That meant that as soon as He realized what God wanted of Him, He did it. Not dutifully, but joyfully. He was excited to find out each new thing His Father desired of Him. It was the most joyous aspect of His life.

I was overwhelmed with the realization that true freedom comes only through reverent submission. When we achieve this, we will delight to do God's will. No more begrudging obedience at any time, only eager, active, delighted obedience. What joy!

The cheese slices? They were left on the plate. My husband won the Changeling game. (His score was 666. How we laughed about that!) I could hardly sleep that night from the excitement of my new clue to the work of the Holy Spirit in my life. Every now and then during the night I woke up and remembered with great joy: "He delighted in the fear of the Lord."

The next day I discovered the following verse:

"The Lord is exalted, for he dwells on high; he will fill Zion with justice and righteousness. He will be the sure foundation for your times, a rich store of salvation and wisdom and knowledge; *the fear of the Lord is the key to this treasure*" (Isaiah 33:5, 6).

How good God is to His children to reveal to us the secrets of His kingdom!

THE NINE-FOLD FRUIT OF THE SPIRIT[2]

One more blessing of the Spirit that I love to think about at the lampstand each morning concerns fruit. God has promised that the fruit of those who are Spirit-filled will be visible. In fact, He said that by seeing the fruit, others will be able to identify us as Christians. The apostle Paul listed the fruit of the Spirit as "love, joy, peace, patience, kindness, goodness, faithfulness, gentleness, and self-control" (Galatians 5:23, 24).

So before I leave the lampstand each morning I ask the Lord to make the fruit of the Spirit visible in my life so that others will know that I am His child.

THE MANY GIFTS OF THE SPIRIT[3]

One more lesson from the lampstand is about the gifts God bestows upon His church to empower us for service. Every person who comes to Christ is given at least one gift, a special ability that he or she can use in service for others. God does not leave us to do our ministry for Him in our own natural power or abilities. He has especially planned for everything needed for ministry: evangelism, teaching, healing, etc. Read the Biblical accounts of this in Romans 12:3-8, 1 Corinthians 12:1-11, Ephesians 4:7-13. For an even richer understanding read the whole chapters listed, noticing that the gifts in each list are not identical, showing us that God provides for every need of the church in every age, in every culture. And it's all based on love, God's love.

I really love the lessons of the lampstand. I learn so much there.

SUMMARY

The fourth step in sanctuary prayer is at the lampstand, or seven-branched candlestick, which represents the fullness of the Holy Spirit. Each morning as I come to the lampstand I state anew my request for the infilling of the Holy Spirit, reminding God of His promise in Luke 11:13. My ability to be filled is, of course, directly related to how emptied I am of sin, accomplished at the cross and the laver.

Isaiah 11:1-5 lists the attributes with which the Holy Spirit filled Jesus and that He desires to give to you and me: wisdom, understanding, counsel, power, knowledge, the fear of the Lord, and righteous judgment. The fear of the Lord (reverent submission) is the key upon which all the others depend.

Isaiah 50:4 is another prophecy of what God the Father and God the Holy Spirit would do for Jesus. Daily the Spirit would awaken Jesus to be taught of God. God would give Him words to speak to the weary.

I ask the Lord to endow me with these same qualities so that I will be enabled to witness for Him. I ask especially for wisdom and wise words to speak. Remember this is not to be prayed just at the beginning of our Christian life. No, this an everyday experience.

The Bible also tells us what we can expect to happen in our lives if we are Spirit filled. The fruit of the Spirit will be visible to those around us:

Love, joy, peace, patience, goodness, kindness, faithfulness, gentleness, and self-control. (Galatians 5:22, 23.)

A Spirit-filled Christian will show by his life that he is a child of God. I pray that this will be my daily experience.

---

[1] E.G. White, *Desire of Ages*, page 224

[2] Because the fruit of the Spirit is a topic often discussed I have only briefly examined it. Yet the importance of fruit in the Christian's life is worthy of deeper study and prayer.

[3] The gifts of the Spirit are often the subject of seminars. These also are worthy of much study and prayer. My chapter on the Holy Spirit was becoming much too long so I left more discussion on these to be found in other places.

CHAPTER SIX

The Table of
His Presence

"Then Jesus declared, 'I am the bread of life.
He who comes to me will never go hungry,
and he who believes in me will never be thirsty.'"
(John 6:35)

The constant light of the lampstand in the earthly
sanctuary revealed a golden table. The table held
twelve loaves of unleavened bread, one loaf for each tribe,
kept continually before the presence of the Lord. Each
Sabbath this bread was replaced with fresh loaves. The
week-old bread, still consecrated by priestly ministration,
was eaten by Aaron and his sons in the sanctuary.

As I come by faith each morning to the table that holds
the bread of life, I long to catch a glimpse of the real table
in the heavenly sanctuary. I wonder just what it holds. My
limited vision cannot reach that far. But God gives me the

opportunity while I still remain on earth, to participate in the life of Jesus. He sets up a table for me to eat from here on earth—even in the presence of my enemies! That was His plan when He set up the earthly sanctuary, and it is still His plan.

We know that the material food we eat becomes the blood and bones of our bodies. The same is true spiritually. The bread of life ingested gives strength and makes action possible in the life of the Christian.

So as I come to the table I come prepared to eat and go into action. One whole day of life stretches before me. For all I know, it may be the last day of my life. I may meet severe trials, enemies, conflicts and challenges of every sort. And so I need to eat and be fortified.

Sometimes we think God is interested only in our spiritual life and not in our daily actions and our work world. I can remember feeling that way. I would work frantically all week, my only spiritual emphasis being my short personal devotions in the morning, family worship after breakfast, worship in the evening with my children, and then a quickie prayer for myself just before hopping into bed for the night.

I was so involved with what I thought of as the 'real' life that spiritual things were very unreal to me during the week. Then the weekend would come around, and I would do my best to 'work up' religious fervor for my Sabbath duties. But God was very gracious to me. He often blessed me greatly on those lovely Sabbaths, in spite of my misconceptions.

When the first of the week arrived, I heaved a sigh of resignation and said, "Well, here we are back in the 'real' world." I still remember the day it dawned on me that I had my worlds confused. My Sabbath world was a portion of the 'real' world; this other world I lived in through the work week was a figment of my imagination! Not that I was to live in physical indolence and devote myself to Bible study and neglect my family. Oh, no! But the physical duties of life, our physical bodies and our daily work, need not be separated from spiritual truths. In fact, spiritual truths are best learned under physical circumstances.

The Lord began to show me the direct relationship between the physical and spiritual in the small details of my life. I remember so well God's patience with me in teaching me elementary lessons.

One day I stood in my son's bedroom doorway as he unpacked for a long-looked-forward-to weekend at home from boarding academy. He tossed a limp, sorry-looking object at me. With the agility of motherhood I caught it, asking, "What ever is this green rag?"

"It's my new velour shirt, Mom. I sent it to the school laundry, and that's what it looks like now. Fix it, will you?"

I took the sad-looking shirt out to the laundry room. I rather doubted my ability to rejuvenate it, but I was eager to try. A quick trip through the gentle cycle of my washer, a few moments of twirling in a warm dryer, and lo, a miracle was performed! Paul's shirt looked as lovely as it had when he first lifted it out of its Christmas wrapping paper.

There in the laundry room I stroked the soft velvet smoothness of the shirt, remembering the rough look of that same garment only a half hour before. The transformation struck a responsive chord in my heart.

"Father in heaven, my life looks like that shirt when it was handed to me by my son. I've tried worldly laundries of personal effort and scientific logic, but it only keeps looking worse and worse. Take my life, Father; fix it, please. You know all the right 'settings.' I need a miracle in my life, too."

My laundry became a chapel as God united for me the spiritual and the physical realms. This is God's purpose for our entire lives—that we recognize the reality of the spiritual through the physical life around us. God showed me two miracles that day—a good-as-new shirt, and a better-than-new life.

God plans that the spiritual act of eating at the table of His presence should prepare us for physical involvement with our world. Now, it may not be the involvement we'd choose for ourselves. The human Jesus would never have chosen the cross. But our commitment is already made when we sit down to eat at the table. It was made at the bronze altar, and we have been growing in the Lord as we prayed.

It was right after Jesus had miraculously multiplied food for more than 5,000 people that He offered His followers the bread of life. They were delighted with His miraculous powers, but even more so with the thought of free food for the rest of their lives. They immediately decided to crown Him king so that they could live in a land of plenty.

Sadly Jesus met with their delegation:

"I tell you the truth, you are looking for me, not because you saw miraculous signs but because you ate the loaves and had your fill. Do not work for food that spoils, but for food that endures to eternal life, which the Son of

Man will give you. On Him God the Father has placed His seal of approval" (John 6:26, 27).

They did not understand what Jesus was saying. They asked for another miracle, one that would equal the manna Moses had called down from heaven. Jesus patiently explained to them that it was not Moses but God the Father who gave the manna. He was also the one who sent the true Bread of Life, of which the manna was only a symbol.

"I am the bread of life," declared Jesus. "He who comes to me will never go hungry, and he who believes in me will never be thirsty" (verse 35).

"I am the living bread that came down from heaven. If a man eats of this bread, he will live forever. This bread is my flesh, which I will give for the life of the world." (verse 51).

The Jews began to argue among themselves. How ridiculous, they exclaimed, "How can this man give us his flesh to eat?" (verse. 52) Just as Nicodemus resisted the physical application of a spiritual truth, so did the Jews.

"Jesus said to them, 'I tell you the truth, unless you eat the flesh of the Son of Man and drink his blood, you have no life in you. Whoever eats my flesh and drinks my blood has eternal life, and I will raise him up at the last day. For my flesh is real food and my blood is real drink. Whoever eats my flesh and drinks my blood remains in me, and I in him. Just as the living Father sent me and I live because of the Father, so the one who feeds on me will live because of me. This is the bread that came down from heaven. Your forefathers ate manna and died, but he who feeds on this bread will live forever'" (Verses 53-58).

The delegation stiffened. This was too much. They actually wanted nothing to do with spiritual things. They were interested only in material possessions and power. Yielding to the demands of this Man would mean changing their entire lifestyle and forsaking their glorious expectations and plans for the future. This was too hard. Total submission to this kind of God? They would lose all individuality. They were not willing.

"From this time many of His disciples turned back and no longer followed him" (verse 66).

This was the turning point in Jesus' ministry. From then on His life was headed straight toward the cross. The one encouraging note of this whole story happened directly after this. Jesus, being human, was naturally sad that so many turned away from him.

"You do not want to leave too, do you?" He asked the twelve disciples (verse 67).

Simon Peter, often spokesman for the group, answered quickly, "Lord, to whom shall we go? You have the words of eternal life. We believe and know that you are the Holy one of God" (see verse 68).

Eating daily of the words of God at the table of His presence is a preparation for service and for sacrifice. When we learn to recognize the reality of spiritual things, the table is a turning point for each of us, too. Will we eat of the Bread of Life and gladly face whatever joy, sorrow, trial, and service the day may hold for us?

When I come to the table each morning I ask God to give me of Himself to prepare me for my day: the housework I must do, the bills I must pay, the plans I need to make for the future, the shopping I need to do, the people I will meet. I want every bit of my life to measure

65

with the life of God. I want even the expression on my face to be godlike.

"With the tongue we praise our Lord and Father, and with it we curse men, who have been made in God's likeness. Out of the same mouth come praise and cursing. My brothers, this should not be. Can both fresh water and salt water flow from the same spring? My brothers, can a fig tree bear olives, or a grapevine bear figs? Neither can a salt spring produce fresh water" (James 3:9-12).

"You cannot drink the cup of the Lord and the cup of demons too; you cannot have a part in both the Lord's table and the table of demons" (1 Corinthians 10:21).

At the table of His presence we have a choice to make, as did the disciples of Jesus. We cannot be half the Lord's and half the world's. We must choose.

At the altar and laver I am forgiven, cleansed, given a new heart, and clothed with the righteousness of Christ. At the lampstand I am endowed with the Holy Spirit for learning and service. Now at the table I am enabled to grow and mature in Christ.

I once read of a well-known man who wrote his autobiography. His daughter read it and was amazed. "If I had not seen his name on the book and recognized names and some incidents, I wouldn't have known it was about my father. His picture of himself is so different from who he really is," she declared.

It is not God's will that the Christian be vacillating and changeable. We profess Christ, and in order to bring honor to His name we must resemble Him in both actions and character. Eating at the table makes our feelings, thoughts, and actions match. The Bible calls this becoming 'partakers of divinity.' This is not an instantaneous transformation, but day by day we grow as a child grows.

"The reception of the Word, the bread from heaven, is declared to be the reception of Christ Himself. As the Word of God is received into the soul, we partake of the flesh and blood of the Son of God. As it enlightens the mind, the heart is opened still more to receive the engrafted Word that we may grow thereby. Man is called upon to eat and masticate the Word; but unless his heart is open to the entrance of that Word, unless he drinks in the Word, unless he is taught of God, there will be a misconception, misapplication, and misinterpretation of that Word.

"As the blood is formed in the body by the food eaten, so Christ is formed within by the eating of the Word of God, which is His flesh and blood. He who feeds upon that Word has Christ formed within, the hope of glory. The written Word introduces to the searcher the flesh and blood of the Son of God; and through obedience to that Word, he becomes a partaker of the divine nature. As the necessity for temporal food cannot be supplied by once partaking of it, so the Word of God must be daily eaten to supply the spiritual necessities.

"As the life of the body is found in the blood, so spiritual life is maintained through faith in the blood of Christ.... By reason of the waste and loss, the body must be renewed with blood, by being supplied with daily food. So there is need of constantly feeding on the Word, the knowledge of which is eternal life. That Word must be our meat and drink. It is in this alone that the soul will find its nourishment and vitality. We must feast upon its precious instruction, that we may be renewed in the spirit of our mind, and grow up into Christ, our living Head." [1]

Normally, we eat physical food more than once a day. What about spiritual food? Will the bread of life that I have partaken of in my morning prayer-time last me all day? Just as God's time is different from ours, so His nourishment is different, too. For one thing, spiritual food, once ingested, is always available again and again. When we read the Word in sincerity of heart, it will often be returned to us in our thoughts with new meanings and blessings. Thus we can eat all day long.

Another wonderful thing about God is His ability to create in us a hunger and thirst for spiritual food so that we will seek out opportunities otherwise squandered to open the Bible and explore its glorious mysteries. It's best not to eat physical food between our regular meals as the stomach needs time to digest the food, but the bread of life, when blended with obedience and action, can be eaten continually and not sicken us.

What I see as the important lesson for me to learn at the table is the lesson of action and obedience. Unless I put the principles I am learning from God's Word into practice I cannot grow. It is important for me to lay before the Lord my physical needs, my plans for the day, and ask for His guidance in my actions.

My favorite verse about the table comes from the familiar twenty-third psalm. David, who was often pursued by enemies, said "You prepare a table for me in the presence of my enemies." Personally I am often beset with enemies of panic, fear, and other besetting sins. But God promises that if I will only look, I will find that He has prepared a table for me, even in the presence of all of these.

Sometimes my enemies are more visible than the ones I have just mentioned. They may be real people out to attack me. But His table is still there. When I come to Him in the morning I first thank Him for the table He has prepared for me in the presence of my enemies. I present before God—right there at the table—my entire day. I ask Him to give me courage and skill to meet each encounter. I tell Him I long to be wholly obedient to His will. I want to have His desires become mine. I want to be a partaker of the divine nature, growing every day.

"His divine power has given us everything we need for life and godliness through our knowledge of him who called us by his own glory and goodness. Through these he has given us his very great and precious promises, so that through them you may participate in the divine nature and escape the corruption in the world caused by evil desires.

"For this very reason, make every effort to add to your faith goodness; and to goodness, knowledge; and to knowledge, self-control; and to self-control, perseverance; and to perseverance, godliness; and to godliness, brotherly kindness; and to brotherly kindness, love. For if you possess these qualities in increasing measure, they will keep you from being ineffective and unproductive in your knowledge of our Lord Jesus Christ. But if anyone does not have them, he is nearsighted and blind, and has forgotten that he has been cleansed from his past sins.

"Therefore, my brothers, be all the more eager to make your calling and election sure. For if you do these things, you will never fall, and you will receive a rich welcome into the eternal kingdom of our Lord and Savior Jesus Christ" (2 Peter 1:10, 11).

"Blessed are those whose strength is in you, who have set their hearts on pilgrimage. As they pass through the Valley of Baca [drought] they make it a place of springs; the autumn rains also cover it with pools. They go from strength to strength till each appears before God in Zion" (Psalm 84:5-7).

I choose pilgrimage at the table each morning, knowing that God in His faithfulness will grant me grace to grow from day to day and at last to be with Him in Paradise. I choose faith, goodness, knowledge, self-control, perseverance, godliness, brotherly kindness, love, determining that I will not be ineffective or unproductive in God's kingdom. I have decided to follow Jesus, and I will not turn back.

A little book called *The Practice of the Presence of God*, by Brother Lawrence, a monk who lived in the early 1600s, has thrilled my soul for years. In this book Brother Lawrence says that he felt just as close to God as he went about his daily work among the pots and pans in the monastery kitchen as he did in the times set aside for meditation and prayer. This was so because he had learned to apply spiritual truths in physical circumstances. His heart was so trained to stay on God that nothing could distract him. I believe that this is an important lesson that the table of His presence has to teach us.

Perhaps you may feel that if you were to follow this plan, it would make you feel strange and unreal, less capable at your work. Not so. Of course, if you try to "put on" godliness on the outside, you'll be strange! But if it grows from the inside out, from eating the bread of life from the sanctuary table, you will only grow more attractive, more real, and more capable at your work.

"When a farmer plows for planting, does he plow continually? Does he keep on breaking up and harrowing the soil? When he has leveled the surface, does he not sow caraway and scatter cummin? Does he not plant wheat in its place, barley in its plot, and spelt in its field? His God instructs him and teaches him the right way. Caraway is not threshed with a sledge, nor is a cartwheel rolled over cummin; caraway is beaten out with a rod, and cummin with a stick. Grain must be ground to make bread; so one does not go on threshing it forever. Though he drives the wheels of his threshing cart over it, his horses do not grind it. All this also comes from the Lord Almighty, wonderful in counsel and magnificent in wisdom" (Isaiah 28:24-29).

All true wisdom comes from God. As we seek a complete relationship with Him, God will teach us added skills in the daily physical work we do. We will become more competent, more skillful, in all that we do.

Just before I leave the table of His presence each morning I remind the Lord that I am wearing the armor He has provided for the Christian to wear to combat the powers of darkness.

"Therefore put on the full armor of God, so that when the day of evil comes, you may be able to stand your ground, and after you have done everything, to stand. Stand firm then, with the belt of truth buckled around your waist, with the breastplate of righteousness in place, and with your feet fitted with the readiness that comes from the gospel of peace. In addition to all this, take up the shield of faith, with which you can extinguish all the flaming arrows of the evil one. Take the helmet of

71

salvation and the sword of the Spirit, which is the word of God. And pray in the Spirit on all occasions with all kinds of prayers and requests. With this in mind, be alert and always keep on praying for all the saints" (Ephesians 6:13-18).

You see, I am going immediately from here to the altar of intercession. This is active service for God, and I need to be outfitted with His armor and protection. I often mention each article listed in Ephesians 6: the belt of truth; the breastplate of Christ's righteousness; the shoes of the readiness of the gospel of peace; the shield of faith; the helmet of salvation; the sword of the Spirit, which is the Word of God. Each day I make the deliberate choice to wear the complete armor that God has provided for me. The promise is that after I have put on that armor I will be able to stand, no matter how hard the attack. I will be able to stand.

There is no magic in a rote recitation of any portion of Scripture. But God has given us the Scriptures worded in imagery that appeals to the heart and mind and helps us to better understand how He works. The picture of armor to protect us helps us to remember biblical principles that God uses in working for our protection from Satan and from our own human weaknesses.

Outfitted in God's armor, I reverently step forward to accept my first active service for others of the new day.

SUMMARY

The fifth step in sanctuary prayer is at the table of showbread—also called the Table of His Presence. The bread represents the body and blood of Jesus, which was offered on the cross, but which is given to mankind for all eternity.

When we eat at His table we become partakers of divinity—that is, His attributes become ours. At the bronze altar, representing the cross of Christ, we are immediately forgiven and accepted as His children. At the table we grow into His likeness. Our thoughts, motives, and actions begin to resemble His. This does not happen suddenly but day by day we become more and more like Him.

As I come to the table each morning I thank God for the table He has prepared for me in the presence of my enemies. Today is an opportunity to live out my faith. The words that I read in the Bible must become action. Obedience is the key word at the Table. In John 6 Jesus talked about the choices that must be made at the Table, the choice either to follow Him completely or turn away. We cannot belong to the Lord and also to the world. This is where we show our faith by our works. Our spiritual life and our physical life must be completely blended.

At the Table I lay all my plans for the day before God to be directed by Him as He sees fit. I accept whatever my day holds—joy, sorrow, trials, service. I want to meet it all just as Jesus would. I want even the expression on my face to be like His.

Just before I leave the Table of His Presence, I remind God that I am wearing His complete armor. Often I mention each piece: the belt of truth, the breastplate of His righteousness, the shoes of the readiness of peace, the shield of His faithfulness, the helmet of my confident expectation of salvation, and the sword of the Spirit in my right hand. I am ready to go to work.

My first work of the day? Intercession at the golden altar.

---

[1] E.G. White, in *Review and Herald*, November 23, 1897.

CHAPTER SEVEN

The Altar of Intercession

"…Because Jesus lives forever, he has a permanent priesthood.
Therefore he is able to save completely
those who come to God through him,
because he always lives to intercede for them."
(Hebrews 7: 24, 25)

The first altar the priests came to in the Mosaic sanctuary was the bronze altar of sacrifice, which represented the sacrifice Jesus was to make on the cross. Now we come to another altar; it represents the continual intercession of Jesus in heaven for His people still on earth.

Only the high priest served at the golden altar of incense in the wilderness sanctuary. Only Jesus serves as our High Priest in the heavenly sanctuary. There He receives the sincere prayers of the contrite. This is the work that Jesus ascended into heaven to do after His resurrection.

"For we do not have a high priest who is unable to sympathize with our weaknesses, but we have one who has been tempted in every way, just as we are—yet was without sin. Let us then approach the throne of grace with confidence, so that we may receive mercy and find grace to help us in our time of need" (Hebrews 4:15, 16).

"Therefore he is able to save completely those who come to God through him, because he always lives to intercede for them" (Hebrews 7:25).

The Israelite priests were not always the best of men. According to the Biblical records, some priests were wicked. Even if they were good men by human standards, they still had to offer sacrifices for their own sins, as well as for those of the people. But Jesus is our perfect priest, with no sin of His own. Surely we can trust Him completely as He intercedes for us in the heavenly sanctuary.

The high priest burned incense specially blended for use in the sanctuary work. This incense represented the perfect intercession of Christ, which He offers continually for us in the heavenly sanctuary. As the fragrance of the incense filled the earthly sanctuary and the whole camp, so the incense of Christ's perfect life, death and resurrection fills the entire universe with the sweet perfume of redemption.

If it were not for the sinless life of Christ, His death and resurrection, no prayer from earth could reach heaven. Our prayers alone have no buoyancy, no power to leave earth. The sweet incense of Christ's life and intercession blends with our feeble earthly prayers, and they are lifted heavenward to the throne of the King of the universe. They have been washed clean of all impurity by the blood of the Lamb of God that was sacrificed for the sins of the world.

The apostle John gave us a glimpse into the heavenly sanctuary and the work that Jesus is doing for us at the altar of incense:

"Another angel, who had a golden censer, came and stood at the altar. He was given much incense to offer, with the prayers of all the saints, on the golden altar before the throne. The smoke of the incense, together with the prayers of the saints, went up before God from the angel's hand" (Revelation 8:3, 4).

The angel mentioned here is symbolic of Jesus Himself, who continually offers our prayers to the Father.

Satan has tried his best to destroy this continual intercession of Christ for mankind. By establishing the Papacy to take the place of the work of the heavenly sanctuary, Satan almost succeeded in hiding from mankind our access through Jesus Christ, to the throne of God. The Papacy set up a human being in place of Jesus, our Intercessor, and claimed for the priests the power to forgive sin. The bread of life, the Bible, was hidden from the common people for centuries. Cruelty, oppression, and persecution marked those years.

As the Reformation broke Satan's spell upon the world, the Scriptures became more and more available to the people. Cleverly Satan became more subtle in his approach. Because of Satan's numerous smokescreens, God's way in the sanctuary is little discussed or understood today, although the Bible is readily available in numerous versions and in hundreds of languages.

Although man cannot forgive sins, Jesus does ask us to join Him in His work of intercession. The Bible gives us examples of godly people who interceded with God for others. Abraham was like that. He cared for his family and friends as a loving father. When God visited Abraham in person and told him of His plans to destroy the wicked city of Sodom, where Abraham's nephew Lot had made his home, Abraham pleaded with God to spare the city. Mercifully, God rescued Lot from destruction in answer to Abraham's prayer.

Moses took on the responsibility of the entire Israelite nation. When God threatened to destroy the rebellious people, Moses reminded God of His promises to Abraham, Isaac, and Jacob, that He would make of them a great nation. God answered Moses' prayer.

It may well be that the above mentioned incidents were given to test Abraham and Moses as to the depth of their love for God. How would we stand such a test? Could it be that we are being tested similarly every day? I have heard it said—but I don't want to believe it—that I can love God only as much as I love the person I love the least. Oh, Lord, give me more love for the unlovely. Make me willing to intercede for them.

God has chosen each Christian to be a priest of His kingdom:

"You also, like living stones, are being built into a spiritual house to be a holy priesthood, offering spiritual sacrifices acceptable to God through Jesus Christ" (1 Peter 2:5).

"But you are a chosen people, a royal priesthood, a holy nation, a people belonging to God, that you may declare the praises of him who called you out of darkness into his wonderful light" (verse 9).

Each of us has a circle of people whom God has given us: family, friends, neighbors. We are responsible not only to represent God to them by our relationship with them, but also to pray for them. As priests of the heavenly sanctuary we can carry them to God in prayer. Our prayers for them allow God to work in their lives in a way in which He could not had we not prayed.

It is not that God lacks the power to intervene in the life of every person in this world. But He has limited himself in order to maintain our individual freedom. He uses no force other than that of love. The love revealed in the cross of Christ is the only force God uses to attract people to Himself.

"But I, when I am lifted up from the earth, will draw all men to myself." (John 12:32)

According to His eternal plan that sin be forever cleansed from the universe, God limits Himself in working with human beings in order to protect individual freedom and to silence Satan's cries of unfairness. Each person is free to choose to follow God or to resist Him. Everyone makes his or her own choices. No one is coerced.

Yet when we pray wholehearted prayers for others, all heaven leaps joyously and freely into operation to answer our prayers. We have by our intercession actually released God to work in a way He was not allowed to before we prayed. Satan's power is broken.

Always remember that true prayer is never our initiative. The Holy Spirit puts God's desires into our hearts, and then we put them into words. Thus we are praying to God by the Spirit's power. We pray this way for others. In fact, it is the only way we can truly pray for anything. When the Holy Spirit impresses us to pray for specific people, then we can pray for them in expectation that God is answering our prayers.

As I come each morning to the altar of incense, it is with the realization that praying for others is the first active service of every Christian. Satan does not desire me to join Jesus in this work. He will do all he can to prevent me from lifting others up before the throne of God. But I come clothed in the righteousness of Christ and wearing His armor. (Read Zechariah 3 for the story of an encounter between Christ and Satan as Joshua the high priest stood praying at the altar of incense.)

I am well protected because Christ is at my right hand offering up the merits of His sweet life before the Father along with my prayers. Not only is Jesus interceding for me, but the Holy Spirit is taking even the desires of my heart that I am unable to put into words and translating them into the language of heaven as prayer (see Romans 8:26, 27). What power for prayer God offers us!

How we pray for others is as individual as we are each unique. Some people have great success with a long list of people for whom they pray every day. God honors their prayers in marvelous ways. However, I am easily burdened and found it too wearying to face a long daily list. Several years ago I decided (under the direction of the Holy Spirit, I believe) to divide my list of people to pray for into seven lists, one for each day of the week. By varying each day's list, I sense the freedom of God.

Of course, I pray daily for my immediate family: husband, children, grandchildren, sisters, nieces and nephews. I pray daily for the sick and others in urgent

80

need, for my close friends, those I am studying the Bible with or am in any small groups with, close friends and those involved in special ministries, individual members of our church, neighbors, those I work with in business, and the leadership of our denomination and of the country, and any others God places upon my heart.

So my short daily list finally ends up with many names. However, there is no reason that we have to do all our praying for others at one time during the day. Sometimes I divide up my list and pray for them occasionally throughout the day. God has no desire that praying for others should become a burden. In fact, it should be a delight and a privilege. So I seek to make it a joy—like talking on the telephone to someone I love about someone else I love. Now, that is never burdensome.

Have you ever wondered about the efficacy of praying for someone you have never met and may never have an opportunity to meet? Surely the solution to that person's need cannot be through your personal influence. Somehow God's plan for us to reach out to share Him with other human beings utilizes a God-given network that is open between all humanity.

The Bible specifies that we are to pray for Christians we have never met, for the heathen, for our rulers. We don't know just how it works, but when we pray for others, God is free to do a work for them which He could not do (because of His own law of individual freedom) if we did not pray. God does not assign busywork. Prayer for others has real merit and is a valuable ministry. Although God knows the needs of all the people we pray for much better than we do, it is His plan that we have a part in lifting their burdens and perhaps even in their salvation. He has given

81

mankind into our hands. It is for our best good and eternal happiness that we reach out in prayer for others.

Once I felt the Spirit's unction to pray for a young man I had never met, the son of members of our church. I had prayed for him faithfully for about three months when the concern for him was lifted from my heart. When later I met him, he was a Bible teacher in one of our academies. I never found out why God put him upon my heart at that special time, but I was glad to support him with my prayers.

"This is the confidence we have in approaching God: that if we ask anything according to his will, he hears us. And if we know that he hears us—whatever we ask—we know that we have what we asked of him.

"If anyone sees his brother commit a sin that does not lead to death, he should pray and God will give him life" (1 John 5:14-16).

I have found that it is possible for something to block my prayers for other people. Do you remember the part the Holy Spirit takes as we pray? He takes the desires of our hearts and presents them before God as prayer. Now, what if I am praying for someone who is having a bad time, but in my heart I am thinking, "Well, it just serves him right; I hope he falls flat on his face"? My words and my heart, or thoughts, are at odds with each other, and my prayer is blocked right there.

It seems to me that it is impossible to truly pray for someone whom you have not forgiven, for someone you look down upon, or someone who is unimportant to you. Whenever the Holy Spirit puts into our hearts the desire to pray for a person, He asks us to forgive that person for anything we hold against him. He shows us how important that person is to Him and asks us to love him. I suspect that being willing to become personally involved with that person should the opportunity arise is another prerequisite for answers to our intercession for others.[1]

Prayer without action is only a form. Remember Jesus' admonition in the Sermon on the Mount:

"Therefore, if you are offering your gift at the altar and there remember that your brother has something against you, leave your gift there in front of the altar. First go and be reconciled to your brother; then come and offer your gift" (Matthew 5:23, 24).

Jesus intimates that a break in a relationship may hinder a prayer—even when it is the other person who has a grudge against me rather than my having a grudge against him. It is my responsibility to do my best to bring about reconciliation. The apostle Peter gave similar instruction to husbands regarding the treatment of their wives:

"Husbands, in the same way be considerate as you live with your wives, and treat them with respect as the weaker partner and as heirs with you of the gracious gift of life, so that nothing will hinder your prayers" (1 Peter 3:7).

Jesus gave His disciples instructions to pray for even their enemies.

"You have heard that it was said, 'Love your neighbor and hate your enemy.' But I tell you: Love your enemies and pray for those who persecute you, that you may be sons of your Father in heaven. He causes His sun to rise on the evil and the good, and sends rain on the righteous and the unrighteous. If you love those who love you, what reward will you get? Are not even the tax collectors doing that? And if you greet only your brothers, what are you doing more than others? Do not even pagans do that? Be

83

perfect, therefore, as your heavenly Father is perfect" (Matthew 5:43-48).

Luke's record of that same discourse ends this way: "Be merciful, just as your Father is merciful" (Luke 6:36).

On one occasion the question was asked of Jesus "Who is my neighbor?" but never, "Who is my enemy?" An enemy seems easily defined: someone who is seeking to harm us either physically, mentally, or emotionally. We know that the greatest enemy, Satan, desires to cause us great discomfort and even seeks to destroy our lives. His final goal is to obtain our eternal annihilation.

I have had few enemies in my life. When I discover one, I seek to remove myself immediately from his presence, and I avoid that person if possible. I find it difficult to pray for him. Do you know why? It is because I do not love him.

God has many lessons for you and me. In order to teach us to love our enemies, He may allow us to discover that someone whom we have always loved and cannot stop loving has become our enemy. Then we will know what it is really like to pray for our enemies. We can share in God's sorrow as He prays for His enemies for it hurts to pray for an enemy you love. But that is the only prayer that reaches heaven, a prayer from a caring heart.

The Lord showed me one day several years ago how closely related to prayer are my thoughts. One day I was washing dishes (my favorite occupation for thinking) and contemplating my family. My mother, still active at 87; several aunts and uncles and their wives, all in their 80s; cousins who are not well; my sisters, who have health problems—all these people might need someone to care for them in the near future.

Unconsciously I began daydreaming: Perhaps John and I should buy a rest home when we retire, and look after them all. Now, for some of my readers that might sound like a practical idea. But I am definitely not the nursing-home-director type. This was strictly a self-pity daydream!

God spoke to me: "Is this what you really want to do with your retirement?"

"Oh no, God!" I exclaimed, shocked at His question. "But perhaps it is what I should do."

At this, God led me to see that every thought of mine is a prayer. (What a joy to know that He is that easy to contact.) But God went on to tell me that He sometimes answers my self-pitying thoughts in the way that I have day-dreamed them. Some of the things in my life that I am unhappy with may, in fact, be my own answered prayers.

I must learn to trust God completely in behalf of the people for whom I am praying. Of course, I should be involved in their lives, but I tend to take responsibility that is not mine. If the time comes when I need to step into care for my family, God will lead me to a workable solution. The weight of the world is not upon my shoulders. Away with self-pity!

As I pondered this conversation with God, I searched my memory for the thoughts that habitually fill my mind. How humbled I am before God and the angels as I realize that even self-indulgent thoughts are preserved in the books of heaven, along with my earnest prayers. Self-pity, resentment, pride, along with my own feeble attempts to make order of my life through daydreaming—what a motley collection of prayers for a Christian!

"Oh, Lord, please forgive my carelessness, erase my self-centered thoughts from the books of heaven. Change my thought patterns, I pray. May I 'take captive every thought to make it obedient to Christ'" (2 Corinthians 10:5).

As my heart and my words and actions (the inside and the outside) become more and more alike, my intercession for others will flow more freely to the throne of God. I can become mighty in intercessory prayer.

"May the words of my mouth and the meditation of my heart be pleasing in your sight, O Lord, my Rock and my Redeemer" (Psalm 19:14).

SUMMARY

The sixth step in sanctuary prayer is at the altar of incense, where Jesus continually intercedes in our behalf. The sweet incense of Christ's perfect life accompanies our prayers and makes them acceptable in heaven.

God asks each of us to become priests, willing to intercede for others. He gives to each of us people for whom we are responsible, both to represent God to them and to carry them to God in prayer.

Because of God's law of freedom, He is limited in what He can do for those who do not ask for His help. But if we pray for them God will do in answer to the prayer of faith what He could not do if we did not ask.[2]

All true prayer must be prayed under the influence of the Holy Spirit. The Holy Spirit takes even the desires and thoughts that we cannot verbalize, puts them into heaven's language, and presents them before the Father as prayer.

There are prerequisites for intercessory prayer: We cannot pray in the Spirit for someone we hold a grudge against or look down upon. We must ask God to give us forgiveness and respect for them as God's children before we can effectively pray for them. But do not neglect to pray for someone because you do not *feel* loving toward them. Remember that love is a choice and as we *choose* to love them with the love God has bestowed upon us even in our sinfulness, God will give us true Christian love for them. We must cultivate a willingness to become involved in their lives if God leads us that way. Prayer without action is only a form.

My thoughts and my words must match in order to reach God in prayer.

---

[1] For more on this subject, read my book, *When We Pray for Others,* Review and Herald Publishing Assoc., 1994.

[2] E. G, White, *The Great Controversy*, page 525.

CHAPTER EIGHT

The Most
Holy Place: Part One

"Then I saw another angel flying in midair,
and he had the eternal gospel to proclaim
to those who live on the earth--to every nation,
tribe, language and people.
He said in a loud voice, 'Fear God and give him glory,
because the hour of his judgment has come.
Worship him who made the heavens,
the earth, the sea and the springs of water."'
(Revelation 14:6, 7)

Behind the second curtain in the earthly sanctuary was the place where the visible presence of God dwelt. The only furniture in this room was the ark of God, which contained the two tablets of the Holy Law written by the finger of God. The ark was covered with the mercy seat and overshadowed by two cherubim of beaten gold.

No careless eye was allowed to see into the Most Holy Place. It was occupied only by God. Once a year, on the Day of Atonement, the high priest entered this room to symbolically remove the sins that had been transferred to the sanctuary through the ministry of the priests over the past year. In the Old Testament sanctuary services, each year represented the whole lifetime of the earth. The Day of Atonement was the day of final reckoning—a day of judgment.

In my Sanctuary Prayer time each morning I look up to the heavenly sanctuary where Jesus is now serving as my High Priest. Even though I live in the great day of judgment, heralded by angels (Revelation 14:6-7), Jesus is still offering repentance and forgiveness. Not only that, but He is interceding in my behalf. He takes my feeble, weak prayers and offers them to the Father as His own desires. I can approach the Most Holy Place with confidence because it is the throne room of God, my Father, and Jesus, my Savior and Friend:

"Therefore, since we have a great high priest who has gone through the heavens, Jesus the Son of God, let us hold firmly to the faith we profess. For we do not have a high priest who is unable to sympathize with our weaknesses, but we have one who has been tempted in every way, just as we are--yet was without sin. Let us then approach the throne of grace with confidence, so that we may receive mercy and find grace to help us in our time of need" (Hebrews 4:14-16).

The presence of God, called the Shekinah, was visible above the curtain that separated the Holy and the Most Holy places, and the incense from the daily intercession wafted over the curtain into the Most Holy Place every day. God was truly living among His people.

God told Moses:

"There, above the cover between the two cherubim that are over the ark of the Testimony, I will meet with you and give you all my commands for the Israelites" (Exodus 25:22).

God met daily with Moses and Aaron in the Holy Place, to instruct them. But yearly—on the Day of Atonement—Aaron alone went into the Most Holy Place, the most intimate and sacred place of all.[1]

In the earthly sanctuary system of worship, ministry done in the courtyard represented aspects of the divine plan of salvation that were accomplished here on earth in the life and death of Jesus. The ministry of the inner apartments of the sanctuary represented what in reality goes on in heaven. When Jesus completed His work on earth and returned to heaven, the courtyard work was accomplished. In fact, no longer was God speaking through the earthly sanctuary and its services. The priests were no longer to be considered His spokesmen. To signify this fact, the curtain dividing the Holy place from the Most Holy was torn from top to bottom at the moment of Jesus' death (Matthew 27:51), baring the Most Holy Place to casual eyes. The presence of God was no longer in the earthly sanctuary. Jesus' followers were individually and as a church to look upward to the heavenly sanctuary in order to communicate with God.

The purpose of the sanctuary ministry—to direct the minds of the people to a coming Redeemer who would die for them upon the cross—was fulfilled. Jesus said, "Just as Moses lifted up the snake in the desert, so the Son of

Man must be lifted up, that everyone who believes in him may have eternal life" (John 3:14, 15). The sacrifices of the earthly sanctuary pointing to the cross were over. Yet even though the ministry of the earthly sanctuary is finished, the cross will be the theme of our stories and songs throughout eternity.

The divine illustration of the sanctuary, given by God to His people, will always be a means of calling our attention to what is going on in the heavenly sanctuary—Jesus' continuing ministry of salvation, intercession and judgment. By faith we daily follow Him into heavenly places.

"But because of his great love for us, God, who is rich in mercy, made us alive with Christ even when we were dead in transgressions—it is by grace you have been saved. And God raised us up with Christ and seated us with him in the heavenly realms in Christ Jesus, in order that in the coming ages he might show the incomparable riches of his grace, expressed in his kindness to us in Christ Jesus" (Ephesians 2:4-7).

"We do have such a high priest, who sat down at the right hand of the throne of the Majesty in heaven, and who serves in the sanctuary, the true tabernacle set up by the Lord, not by man" (Hebrews 8:1, 2).

Instead of relying upon human priests to connect humanity with God, God now calls each of us to be priests, leading others to Him:

"To him who loves us and has freed us from our sins by his blood, and has made us to be a kingdom and priests to serve his God and Father--to him be glory and power for ever and ever! Amen" (Revelation 1:5, last part).

When Jesus moved from the Holy Place to the Most Holy Place in the heavenly sanctuary to begin the final phase of the salvation plan, the Most Holy Place experience was opened up to every born-again Christian.[2] This is a secret God is seeking to share with each of us. He is asking us to cooperate with him as He prepares a people who will be able to reveal His glory to the universe and live with Him throughout eternity.

The sanctuary illustration can be divided into 3 phases:

- The courtyard ministry, representing justification, being made right with God
- The Holy Place ministry, representing sanctification, growing in Christ
- The Most Holy Place ministry, representing glorification, being made ready for translation.

In my books I seldom use theological terms. I try to put spiritual concepts into more contemporary language, easily understood by the average reader. However, justification, sanctification and glorification are all basic scriptural terms for the steps of salvation. As we are seeking to understand God's secrets, hidden in the Bible, perhaps using these Biblical terms may help us see the steps of God's personal work in our behalf more clearly.

When I first began to grasp a little of the vastness of the plan of redemption and the opportunities for exploration through Sanctuary Prayer, I understood little of what Jesus is actually doing in the Most Holy Place, the place of judgment. I realized, of course, that Jesus was continuing His ministry of forgiveness and cleansing lives from sin. Although I knew the sacrifice for sin was complete at the cross, obviously there is more to erasing sin from the universe for eternity than just this one event. If the complete work of salvation was *finished* at the cross, why are we still on earth 2000 years later? I came to see that though the *sacrifice* was complete at the cross, the cross was only the beginning of Christ's ministry as our High Priest. The work of Jesus as High Priest is yet to be completed. Now it is time for His final ministry, the Hour of His Judgment is come.

My problem was that I considered the pre-advent judgment of the Most Holy Place to be wholly a legal work of investigation of the books of heaven to see who was saved and who was lost so Jesus would know whom to take to heaven. When the book work was completed, Jesus could return to earth. It had always puzzled me that I was supposed to be excited about this investigation and eager to tell others. The reality was that I dreaded it and saw nothing in it to share.

But slowly, through Sanctuary Prayer, I began to see a new picture: As Jesus our Judge reviews our life page in the books of heaven[3] He is not looking for a way to condemn us. He is looking for a way to save us. God knows by heart all that is written in His books. His purpose for review at this time in the pre-advent judgment, is to make sure the entire universe sees how the plan of salvation is working in our lives.

Part of Jesus' work as Intercessor and Judge is to reveal to us the sins in our lives, including the ones hidden deep in our hearts. Motives as well as actions are under review. The standard of God's judgment is always the Ten Commandment law, spoken audibly by God on Mount Sinai, written with His own finger on the two tablets of stone stored in the ark of the testimony in the earthly sanctuary, and recorded by Moses in the Holy Scriptures. These commandments reveal the basic character of God, not only in our world but throughout the universe. God always acts according to these laws. Although Satan has done his best to change or cover up these commandments (see Daniel 7:25) God's laws can never be destroyed. Heaven holds the originals in the ark of the heavenly sanctuary. In the book of Revelation Christ's inauguration as our Judge is heralded by a dramatic scene from the heavenly sanctuary:

"Then God's temple in heaven was opened, and within his temple was seen the ark of his covenant. And there came flashes of lightning, rumblings, peals of thunder, an earthquake and a great hailstorm" (Revelation 11:19).[4]

The Ten Commandments were given as a protection for humanity. They are meant to heal not hurt. It was because of the broken law that Jesus bore our sins on the cross. The penalty for mankind's sin was paid by Jesus. Justice was upheld. Jesus offers us the white robe of His righteousness to wear and the power of the Holy Spirit to give us victory over every inherited and cultivated tendency to sin. All He needs from us is our cooperation, the choice to choose life over death. His judgment work is to remove sin from our hearts so that it can be removed from the books in heaven. *The work of judgment done in heaven to remove sin is dependent upon work done on earth in individual hearts.*

How much God loves us! Every part of our acceptance of God's free gift of eternal life is dependant upon our cooperation. That is free will—a part of God's basic character. When we co-operate with Him, we can find hope, joy, and peace in the pre-advent judgment. We will rejoice in the judgment because God is on our side. Yes, there is *good news in the judgment.*

"The great plan of redemption, as revealed in the closing work for these last days, should receive close examination. The scenes connected with the sanctuary above should make such an impression upon the minds and hearts of all that they may be able to impress others. All need to become more intelligent in regard to the work of the atonement, which is going on in the sanctuary above. When this grand truth is seen and understood, those who hold it will work in harmony with Christ to prepare a people to stand in the great day of God, and their efforts will be successful. By study, contemplation, and prayer God's people will be elevated above common, earthly thoughts and feelings, and will be brought into harmony with Christ and His great work of cleansing the sanctuary above from the sins of the people. Their faith will go with Him into the sanctuary, and the worshipers on earth will be carefully reviewing their lives and comparing their characters with the great standard of righteousness. They will see their own defects; they will also see that they must have the aid of the Spirit of God if they would become qualified for the great and solemn work for this time which is laid upon God's ambassadors." [5]

This quotation summarizes the important opportunities we each have as we enter by faith into the Most Holy Place in heaven. As we understand Jesus' work better, we can cooperate with Him as He purifies our lives and hearts of sin. This will prepare us to reach out and share this good news with the world.

WHAT DOES THIS MEAN TO ME
AS I COME TO THE MOST HOLY PLACE
IN MY MORNING SANCTUARY PRAYER?

What it meant to me when I first began sanctuary praying was that I could come into the actual presence of God each morning and expect to hear Him speak to me. Knowing that this was God's desire and plan increased my faith immediately and delighted my heart.

God honored my faith and expectations and began to show me how He was working for me in the Most Holy Place in heaven. I have related in the book *Practical Pointers to Personal Prayer* (Review and Herald Publishing Association, 1989) how He began showing me what He was like and pointing out the weak points in my character. What a contrast! But how I loved hearing His voice.

(When I say I hear God's voice, please understand that I do not hear an audible voice. I hear him in the same way that He speaks to all of us, through the inward voice of the Holy Spirit. As far as the Bible tells us, the Son of God, when He became a man, heard the audible voice of God only three times: at His baptism, on the mount of transfiguration, and in the temple just before His crucifixion. In His daily life Jesus was content to hear with the inward voice of the Holy Spirit just as we do.)

For those who may dread facing God's judgment, I assure you that the joy far outweighs the pain. Of course, it is not pleasant to find out that there is absolutely nothing good about yourself except that God loves you. But how delightful to be assured of that very great love and His plan to ready you for His second coming. If you are wallowing in self-pity over your revealed sins, you have been listening to a voice other than God's. God's voice brings you joy. Satan's voice brings you hopelessness and despair.

In the next chapter I will briefly outline how I understand Jesus' ministry in the Most Holy Place relates to each of us personally as we near the end of time. Looking back to the earthly illustration, the Day of Atonement was a day of judgment. Before the day was finished, the camp of Israel was completely cleansed from all sin. Those who were unrepentant were expelled from the camp.

We can expect that this same work will be accomplished in the church as the real day of at-one-ment closes. We can either cooperate with God in this work or ignore it and remain in lukewarm complacency. It is our choice. Either way, the work will be completed before earth's probation closes. This choice determines our final destiny.

If we willingly unite with Jesus in this special judgment work, His presence will change us day by day into people who will be safe to save eternally:

- We will worship God in spirit and in truth
- We will join Him in intercession for our families, our friends, and the world
- We will reach out in service to others
- We will teach righteousness

If we ignore God's final warning, Jesus will weep as He says to us, as He said to ancient Israel, "Why will you die? I take no pleasure in the death of anyone" (Ezekiel 18:31, last part). Matthew records a parable told by Jesus, of the final separation of the wicked and the righteous. In the parable Jesus says that He will be forced to say to those who have chosen not to identify wholly with Him, "Depart from me, you who are cursed, into the eternal fire prepared for the devil and his angels" (Matthew 25:41).

God is longsuffering and patient with us. Right now He is giving us the opportunity to join with Him as He prepares a people to light up the whole world with His glory. The choice is ours. Jesus' words to the church of Laodicea in Revelation 3 are His counsel to us today:

"These are the words of the Amen, the faithful and true witness, the ruler of God's creation. I know your deeds, that you are neither cold nor hot. I wish you were either one or the other! So, because you are lukewarm--neither hot nor cold--I am about to spit you out of my mouth. You say, `I am rich; I have acquired wealth and do not need a thing.' But you do not realize that you are wretched, pitiful, poor, blind and naked. I counsel you to buy from me gold refined in the fire, so you can become rich; and white clothes to wear, so you can cover your shameful nakedness; and salve to put on your eyes, so you can see.

"Those whom I love I rebuke and discipline. So be earnest, and repent. Here I am! I stand at the door and knock. If anyone hears my voice and opens the door, I will come in and eat with him, and he with me.

"To him who overcomes, I will give the right to sit with me on my throne, just as I overcame and sat down with my Father on his throne (Revelation 3:14-21).

Every morning as I close my prayer time I invite God to walk with me through my day.

Oh, I love dwelling in the Most Holy Place!

THE MOST HOLY PLACE: PART ONE

SUMMARY

Behind the second curtain in the earthly sanctuary, the Most Holy Place where God's visible glory dwelt was secluded from even the eyes of the priest workers in the sanctuary. Only the high priest dared to go into the Most Holy Place—and then only once a year on the Day of Atonement.

The sanctuary illustration can be divided into 3 phases:

- The courtyard ministry, representing justification, being made right with God
- The Holy Place ministry, representing sanctification, growing in Christ
- The Most Holy Place ministry, representing glorification, being made ready for translation

God's plan is that we will be able to find the parallels between the Day of Atonement and the final work of Jesus' ministry in the Most Holy Place of the heavenly sanctuary. During the judgment His work is to compare our lives with His Holy Law and point out to us the areas in which we have not wholly yielded our lives to Him so that He can heal us and prepare us to be among those who light up the whole world with the glory of God.

If we willingly unite with God in this special judgment work His presence will change us day by day into people who will be safe to save eternally:

- We will worship God in spirit and in truth
- We will join Jesus in intercession for our families, our friends, and the world
- We will reach out in service to others
- We will teach righteousness

The curtain between the Holy and the Most Holy Place was torn from top to bottom by an unseen hand as Jesus died on the cross. The Most Holy Place is now accessible to all who accept the sacrifice of Jesus in their behalf. As priests of the Most High God, we may, by faith, live in the Most Holy Place.

In my daily Sanctuary Prayer I seek to cooperate with Jesus in His judgment work in my life. When God points out sin in my life, I confess it as sin, and willingly accept whatever it takes to cleanse me.

Praise God for the lessons in the Most Holy Place!

---

[1] To learn more about the wilderness sanctuary services, study the Old Testament books of Exodus, Leviticus, Numbers, and Deuteronomy and the New Testament book of Hebrews. An excellent commentary on this subject is *The Cross and Its Shadow*, by Stephen N. Haskell,, originally published in 1914, but reprinted in paperback in 1970 by Southern Publishing Assoc., Tennessee, and still available in Adventist Book Centers. For a great textbook on the subject of God's complete plan of redemption from sin, read *The Great Controversy*, by E. G. White, Pacific Press Publishing Association, Mountain View, California, now in Nampa, Idaho.

[2] To learn more about when Jesus moved to the final phase of His ministry, symbolized by the earthly Day of Atonement, study the prophecies of Daniel and Revelation. The two books listed in the endnote above are also good commentaries on this subject. A more current book on this subject is *1844 Made Simple*, by Clifford Goldstein, Pacific Press, Publishing Association, Boise, Idaho.

[3] The Bible talks about record books kept in heaven. *The Book of Life:* Psalm 69:28; Philippians 4:3; Revelation 3:5. *The book of Remembrance:* Malachi 3:16.

[4] For more on this subject read E. G. White, *The Great Controversy*, chapter 25, "The Law Immutable", pages 433-460.

[5] E. G. White, *Testimonies,* volume 5, page 575.

CHAPTER NINE

The Most
Holy Place: Part Two

*"He will keep you strong to the end,
so that you will be blameless on the day
of our Lord Jesus Christ.
God, who has called you into fellowship
with his Son Jesus Christ our Lord, is faithful."
(1 Corinthians !:8, 9)*

In the last chapter I introduced you to the Most Holy Place and the ministry of Jesus as our Judge, in addition to His continuing ministry of salvation: repentance and forgiveness of sin, and intercession. In this chapter I will discuss how the pre-advent judgment becomes personal as God works in our individual lives.

God has a design for a perfect character for each of us and He is working that design out in us through the judgment. He promises to see the job completed. If we cooperate with Him in His judgment ministry we will find peace on this earth and joy in contemplating His second coming. Furthermore, we will be a part of the group who light up the world with God's glory.

Although the judgment has a universal scope, yet it is also very personal and practical. It fits our daily life. In this chapter I am putting into words the way I see the personal side of the pre-advent judgment, how it has become real to me.

The apostle Paul says: "Being confident of this, that he who began a good work in you will carry it on to completion until the day of Christ Jesus" (Philippians 1: 6). This verse is a promise to me that God is at work in my life and as long as I continue cooperating with Him I can be certain that I will be found ready at His appearing.

As I made the choice to cooperate with God in the pre-advent judgment as He prepares me for eternity, I had some big questions:

If the last generation of human beings to live on earth must go through the steps of judgment in order to be safe to save in God's kingdom, what about the millions who lived before us? How were they prepared to face God in the judgment?

When I asked God about this, He opened up my mind to see a little bit more of His plan. The cross is the focal point of eternity. Before the cross, people were saved by faith in the coming sacrifice just as surely as those who lived after Jesus actually lived and died. The shadow of the cross falls backward as well as forward.

This is a spiritual truth not true in our physical lives. God works backward as well as forward. He can answer our prayers before we pray them. The same is true with all of Christ's High Priestly work. It was applied by faith to every person who wholeheartedly accepted Him.

Now we come to the pre-advent judgment: Life records of everyone who professed to serve the Most High God are being investigated at this time. This investigation works backward as well as forward. All mankind is sanctified by faith in the judgment work of Jesus. Enoch and Elijah were prepared to live in a perfect heaven, without tasting death, by faith in the final judgment work of our High Priest, Jesus. By faith their lives were examined by God, by themselves, and by the universe, just as we must be.

The difference, of course, is that the final generation has a special work granted to no other generation. Our example before the world and the universe is the last display of God's glory that this doomed world will ever see. God designs that His last generation will delight even the universe by their purity and godlikeness. We are to be the display of His splendor.

When I first began cooperating with Jesus as He examined my life, I knew very little about the personal aspects of the judgment. I was surprised at His personal interest, delighted that He considered me important enough to spend time with me, and horrified at the depths of my defilement.[1] But I began to see that this experience is necessary so that we can cooperate with Jesus in His work of cleansing us from sin. His purpose is to reveal our sins to us so that we may repent of them. Although I must search my own heart and life that I may recognize my sin and renounce it, it is the Holy Spirit who points it out to me and gives me the opportunity to view sin as God does. He waits for me to agree with Him. He will save no one without their wholehearted consent and cooperation.

103

Life on this earth will not go on and on endlessly. Humans tend to believe that they are immortal: "First of all, you must understand that in the last days scoffers will come, scoffing and following their own evil desires. They will say, 'Where is this "coming" he promised? Ever since our fathers died, everything goes on as it has since the beginning of creation.' But they deliberately forget that long ago by God's word the heavens existed and the earth was formed out of water and with water. By water also the world of that time was deluged and destroyed. By the same word the present heavens and earth are reserved for fire, being kept for the day of judgment and destruction of ungodly men" (2 Peter 3:3-7).

I began to understand that God is very fair. We are all saved in the same way, by the same standard of His holy law. However, those who lived when Jesus lived on earth were privileged to walk and talk with God in person as a Man. The disciples of Jesus witnessed His miracles, His crucifixion and resurrection. They watched Him return to heaven. What an honor! We who live in the last days of earth's history will be a part of many amazing events. We will receive the Latter Rain of the Holy Spirit to enable us to preach the gospel with great power. Each generation has its own privileges and special blessings. It is time for us to cooperate with Jesus in His work of judgment, thanking Him that we are privileged to live in the time of the pre-advent judgment.

It has helped me in understanding God's final work of judgment in my life to divide the pre-advent judgment into three distinct phases, each an aspect of His efforts in my behalf:

- Investigation
- Discipline
- Instruction

These three phases, or areas, of judgment, intertwine and mingle in our life experience, they do not stand alone, but understanding each of them separately, helps me to accept and cooperate with what God is doing in my life.

INVESTIGATION

This first phase, investigation, also has three parts:

- God's inspection, not only of my actions, but also of my thoughts and motives
- My heart-searching examination of myself
- Intelligent creatures of the universe examine my life.

Although the first two elements of investigation: God's investigation of me, and my examination of myself, are the most important to me personally, I want to discuss the third part first because I believe this will give us a larger picture of God's plan, not only for our world but also for the universe. Then we can go on to what involves us more personally.

THE UNIVERSE EXAMINES ME

"We have been made a spectacle to the whole universe, to angels as well as to men" (1 Corinthians 4:9, last part).

The thought jolted me a bit at first, thinking of my life being viewed—and even examined—by the numberless sinless beings of the universe, as well as by Satan and the fallen angels. But if God is to have a perfectly happy and sinless universe throughout eternity, peopled with intelligent creatures, then all the questions concerning His character must be answered now, before this world ends and production of the new world goes into high gear.

Since I claim to be God's child and have taken the name Christian as my own, then my life must reveal whether God's plan of redemption from sin actually works. Many plans seem good on the drawing board, but the real test comes when they are put into practical action.

So the angels and other intelligent beings in the universe who have never sinned, watch eagerly to see if God's plan really works in my life. By now, of course, they have seen it work notably in the lives of such people as Enoch, Noah, Abraham, Moses, David, Paul, and unnamed others—although pitifully few in comparison with the total number of the world's inhabitants. God Himself became a man; as Jesus He gave a perfect example of how the plan can work in sinful humanity.

It is important that God be able to defend Himself when He gives me eternal life. It must be apparent that I have accepted Jesus' sacrifice for my sins, received a new heart, been endowed with the power of the Holy Spirit, and am living His life of obedience. Citizens of the universe must be sure that I will not create a disturbance in eternity. It is important to their future happiness.

God's honor rests upon my life. It is an awesome thought to realize that when I sin I place God in a bad light before His universe. "Oh, Lord, forgive me for the many times I have carelessly dishonored you, not only before my world, but before the universe."

"His intent was that now, through the church, the manifold wisdom of God should be made known to the

106

rulers and authorities in the heavenly realms, according to his eternal purpose which he accomplished in Christ Jesus our Lord" (Ephesians 3:10, 11).

So, you see, it is not only me, but you also—all who profess Christ's name, Christian. We are on display before the universe.

As to Satan. I hate to think of him and his imps viewing my life. But they do. And whenever 1 fall into sin, they taunt Jesus and the holy angels:

"Look at Carrol," they exult. "Isn't she supposed to be one of your saints? She's no better than our followers. Worse than some. The plan of redemption does not work. It is impossible to obey God's laws. She is evidence of it."

But the critics are always silenced by two things. First, Jesus lived a perfect sinless life in a human body. The plan worked. Second, I have confessed my sin and repented, and am relying entirely upon Jesus for my salvation. The plan is working still.

So much for the universe. Now, what is happening between God and mankind (me) in this final investigation?

GOD'S EXAMINATION OF ME

"I the Lord search the heart and examine the mind, to reward a man according to his conduct, according to what his deeds deserve" (Jeremiah 17:10).

"For a man's ways are in full view of the Lord, and he examines all his paths" (Proverbs 5:21).

Sometimes we fear the eyes of God upon us. I remember that when a group of my cousins, my sisters, and I, played together in our yard, my grandmother could often be seen peering out the window. I began to realize that whenever we saw Grandma looking out the window at us, we were almost certain to be called in to account for misbehavior. We resented her spying on us. We sometimes feel that way about God.

I was delighted to find that although God notes our misbehavior, yet His reasons for examining us is not to get us into trouble. No, *it is to get us out of trouble*:

"The eyes of the Lord are on the righteous and *his ears are attentive to their cry*" (Psalm 34:15, italics mine).

"For the eyes of the Lord range throughout the earth to *strengthen* those whose hearts are fully committed to him" (2 Chronicles 16:9, middle part, italics, mine).

As God examines us in the judgment it is to point out our sins, the areas in which we are weak, and to forgive and strengthen us so that we can be effective and happy Christians.

MY EXAMINATION OF MYSELF

"Let us examine our ways and test them, and let us return to the Lord" (Lamentations 3:40).

"Examine yourselves to see whether you are in the faith; test yourselves. Do you not realize that Christ Jesus is in you—unless, of course, you fail the test?" (2 Corinthians 13:5).

While it is important that I examine myself, I must remember that God's scrutiny of me always reveals truth, while my examination of myself probably will be faulty. Therefore, I must always test my search by the Word of God. (I'll talk more about tests in the next chapter.)

When I can accept God's conclusions as wholly true I can repent and receive forgiveness and cleansing. God is in the work of at-one-ment, making us at one with Him in our desire for righteousness. The results of my heart

108

search must become identical to Jesus' judgment in order for me to feel the need for repentance. I must say "Yes!" to Jesus. He must have my complete cooperation before He can complete His loving work of judgment for me and in me.

One word of caution as we go about the work of examining ourselves:

"'Examine yourselves to see whether you are in the faith" (2 Corinthians 13:5). Some conscientious souls, on reading this, immediately begin to criticize their every feeling and emotion. But this is not correct self-examination. It is not the petty feelings and emotions that are to be examined. The life, the character, is to be measured by the only standard of character, God's holy law. The fruit testifies to the character of the tree. Our works, not our feelings, bear witness of us.

"The feelings, whether encouraging or discouraging, should not be made the test of the spiritual condition. By God's Word we are to determine our true standing before Him." [2]

DISCIPLINE

The second way that God works in judgment is through discipline, which has two parts:

- Cutting
- Healing

Trials, persecution, and suffering are the tools that God uses in disciplining us:

"My son, do not despise the Lord's discipline and do not resent his rebuke, because the Lord disciplines those he loves, as a father the son he delights in" (Proverbs 3:11, 12).

After the above verses are quoted in Hebrews 12, Paul goes on to comment:

"Endure hardship as discipline; God is treating you as sons. For what son is not disciplined by his father? If you are not disciplined (and everyone undergoes discipline), then you are illegitimate children and not true sons. Moreover, we have all had human fathers who disciplined us and we respected them for it. How much more should we submit to the Father of our spirits and live! Our fathers disciplined us for a little while as they thought best; but God disciplines us for our good, that we may share in his holiness. No discipline seems pleasant at the time, but painful. Later on, however, it produces a harvest of righteousness and peace for those who have been trained by it" (verses 7-11).

Hosea speaks of both the *cutting* and the *healing:* "Come, let us return to the Lord. He has torn us to pieces but he will heal us; he has injured us but he will bind up our wounds" (Hosea 6:1).

Isaiah also mentions the cutting and healing as coming from the hand of the Lord: "...The Lord binds up the bruises of his people and heals the wounds he inflicts" (Isaiah 30:26, last part).

All my life 1 heard that trials were good for me. But I ignored this admonition because it didn't fit the dreams I had. I could handle hardship and hard work; I recognized this as the lot of all the poor of earth. But when I underwent severe trials I cried and wept like a spoiled child. I considered myself a favored child of God who would always be pampered.

110

As I examine my childhood I discover where those unrealistic expectations took root. As a child I had several things going for me. I was sick a good share of my childhood and so only needed to look pale or tired in order to get out of any work around the house. Because of my illness I could not attend school often, but since I was naturally studious, I managed to keep up with my classes in our small church school. I received a lot of delightful attention because of my love of learning and my sickness. I began to feel that I was a very special child.

I did not completely outgrow these unrealistic expectations. When I became an adult, life continued to go beautifully for me. My health was better and I didn't mind hard work. I had a loving husband and four children who brought me great joy. Although as a pastor's family we moved often, I loved decorating a home, and we always found a house just a little nicer than the one we had moved from. I had a job I enjoyed. I looked forward to the future. In other words, I expected that my life would only become better and better. I was still the pampered child.

THE DISCIPLINE OF CUTTING

As time went by, reality set in. God began His cutting discipline for my best good. How bewildered I was as my life changed drastically. Yet it was just this experience that led me to a deeper relationship with God through Sanctuary Prayer. I can only be thankful for God's loving discipline.

For the first time in my life I am learning to look at myself realistically. It isn't a pretty sight. But God loves me. Oh, He loves me so much! He is not finished with me yet.

Isaiah tells us that these trials and afflictions can actually become our teachers:

"O people of Zion, who live in Jerusalem, you will weep no more. How gracious he will be when you cry for help! As soon as he hears, he will answer you. Although the Lord gives you the bread of adversity and the water of affliction, your teachers will be hidden no more; with your own eyes you will see them. Whether you turn to the right or to the left, your ears will hear a voice behind you, saying, 'This is the way; walk in it.'" (Isaiah 30:19-21).

THE DISCIPLINE OF HEALING

The second part of discipline—after the cutting—is the healing, which God accomplishes with His sweet comfort, peace, and joy. The cutting would be unbearable if it were not for the joy of healing. Often God applies a cool application of comfort to the cut immediately.

One day I was doing dishes at the kitchen sink, contemplating the cutting God was doing in my life. One sorrow in my life just seemed to swell and roll into another sorrow. There was no end to grief.

"I can't bear any more, Father," I cried. "Surely this is enough. I cannot stand any more grieving." God answered immediately.

"Why are you complaining, Carrol, when I consider you worthy to share in My suffering?"

I paused in my dishwashing. Me, worthy to share in His suffering?

"Oh, Father," I breathed, "this is Your suffering?" I gulped down the sorrow that clogged my throat and

112

smiled. "Forgive me for complaining," I said. I remembered Peter's comments about suffering: "But rejoice that you participate in the sufferings of Christ, so that you may be overjoyed when his glory is revealed" (1 Peter 4:13).

Paul also said: "Now if we are children, then we are heirs —heirs of God and co-heirs with Christ, if indeed we share in his sufferings in order that we may also share in his glory" (Romans 8:17).

I always thought that in order to share in the sufferings of Christ I would have to be put in prison for my faith in God, or be persecuted by my neighbors because of my Christian lifestyle. My present sorrow seemed unrelated to God. Yet God assured me that whenever His child suffers, He suffers, too.

The sweetness of His comfort brightened my life for many a day. Perhaps I *am* a favored child.

It is true, we are all His favored children—and how He loves His children! That is why we must expect and welcome trials, sorrows, and persecution, always calling to mind that healing is the other side of trials. Whenever there is a trial, God's comfort is always available.

INSTRUCTION

The third part of judgment is instruction which has four parts:

- God teaches us about Himself
- God teaches us about ourselves and others
- God teaches us doctrine and prophecy
- God gives us wisdom to become capable workmen in our daily life.

God has much to teach us if we will only listen. As I come each morning to the Most Holy Place, I come eager for instruction. *God's special plan for His last-day people is that they know and understand Him better than any people before them.* This will not happen just because we wish it to be so. No man or woman is successful in an earthly enterprise without earnestness, diligence, and perseverance. Hours are spent in preparation. The whole heart is in the endeavor. Can we think it will take less than that to prepare us for the kingdom of God? God's instruction will mean nothing to us unless we are dedicated to learning. Listen to the words of God spoken through the wisest man who ever lived:

"My son, if you accept my words and store up my commands within you, turning your ear to wisdom and applying your heart to understanding, and if you call out for insight and cry aloud for understanding, and if you look for it as for silver and search for it as for hidden treasure, then you will understand the fear of the Lord and find the knowledge of God. For the Lord gives wisdom, and from his mouth come knowledge and understanding. He holds victory in store for the upright, he is a shield to those whose walk is blameless, for he guards the course of the just and protects the way of his faithful ones. Then you will understand what is right and just and fair—every good path. For wisdom will enter your heart, and knowledge will be pleasant to your soul. Discretion will protect you, and under standing will guard you" (Proverbs. 2:1-11).

We will not understand the secrets the Lord wants to reveal to us until we are willing to give everything we have to know them. Jesus longs to teach us, and He has so

114

much to say. He is only waiting for us to listen. "He who has ears, let him hear," is still His counsel to us today

GOD TEACHES US THE TRUTH ABOUT HIMSELF

The instruction that God has for us is as varied as we are different from one another. Most important of all, He wants us to know and understand what He is like. He will reveal this through His Word, through nature, and through loving relationships with other people. Not until we have a growing picture of who God is, can we begin to be like Him.

God's goal for His people and for this planet is that the earth will be filled with the knowledge of the Lord (Isaiah 11:9, last part). The truth about God will thrill our hearts and allow us to worship in a way that would be impossible without a deep understanding of His character.

Worldly wisdom and experience often block our comprehension of God. We see Him humanly instead of divinely, and our proud hearts limit our willingness to allow the Holy Spirit to stretch our minds to enable us to view the truth about Him. We must humble ourselves as little children before Him and allow Him to teach us what He is really like.

GOD TEACHES US THE TRUTH ABOUT OURSELVES AND HELPS US UNDERSTAND OTHERS

Next He shows us what we are really like underneath the facade we have built for ourselves. Sometimes it seems to us that this search is not safe. We are afraid that God is seeking to destroy us. The truth is that He wants to show us His wonderful plans for our future.

He teaches us the value of each human being around us so that we will treat them tenderly and lovingly. Jesus Himself said: "A new command I give you: Love one another. As I have loved you, so must you love one another. All men will know that you are my disciples if you love one another" (John 13:34, 35).

The apostle John learned this lesson from Jesus so well that he spoke often of the necessity of loving each other:

"Anyone who claims to be in the light but hates his brother is still in the darkness. Whoever loves his brother lives in the light, and there is nothing in him to make him stumble" (1 John 2:9, 10).

"We know that we have passed from death to life, because we love our brothers. Anyone who does not love remains in death" (1 John 3:14).

Learning to love God, ourselves, and others is an ongoing lesson. It is only as we begin to experience the love of God for us personally that we can view ourselves and others realistically. God graciously gives us ample opportunities to practice loving in our daily interaction with others.

GOD TEACHES US TRUE DOCTRINE AND PROPHECY

He opens to us Bible concepts of true doctrine and prophecy. God cannot be honored by error or falsehood; only the truth brings glory to Him. Because of the availability of the Bible ignorance is no excuse. It is God's desire to teach each hungry, seeking soul true doctrine and to reveal the mysteries of prophecy.

We can expect and know that He will teach us truth in the Most Holy Place. It is the responsibility and privilege of each child of God to search the Bible in order to understand truth. Especially as we near the end of time, it is important that we familiarize our minds with God's final warnings and promises so that we will be able to stand firmly in the place He has planned for us. Each revelation that we receive from Him is a promise of further light and understanding. It is His delight to give.

GOD GIVES US THE WISDOM TO BECOME CAPABLE AND CONSCIENTIOUS WORKMEN

He teaches us that everything we do in our physical life should be done well. The wisest man ever known, King Solomon, advises that "whatever your hand finds to do, do it with all your might" (Ecclesiastes 9:10, first part).

The prophet Isaiah discusses the farmer and his wisdom in planting and harvesting. He concludes with: "...His God instructs him and teaches him the right way. ...All this also comes from the Lord Almighty, wonderful in counsel and magnificent in wisdom" (Isaiah 28:24-29).

God desires to give us that same counsel and wisdom to do all our work well. Surely Christians should be the most thorough and accomplished workers in the world!

About six years ago in a city not far from where I live a church congregation built a beautiful new church. How they delighted in its beauty! But a few months ago the buildings were condemned by county inspectors as unsafe to use anymore. What a shock to that congregation! Their lovely new church was unsafe because the builders did not faithfully follow the specifications of the architectural plans and used inferior materials. God was publicly dishonored in that city by careless Christian workmen.

No matter what we do for a life work, God is honored by how conscientiously we do it. Jesus spent a number of

117

years in the carpenter shop helping His father, Joseph. Surely Jesus was a careful and faithful workman. Jesus is our example whether we are working as health professionals, teaching school, taking care of the elderly, cleaning houses, working as a secretary, or a CEO of a large company.

The instruction from the Most Holy Place is not limited to prayer time. It is our privilege to dwell in the Most Holy Place continually by faith. As we read His word, as we work, as we contemplate nature, God will teach us.

Some of our instruction will come as a surprise. But much of what God teaches us should come because we have prepared for it. God wants us to plan time in our day to spend in Bible study, meditation, and prayer. God's instruction for us comes most often from the words of Scripture.

"None but those who have fortified the mind with the truths of the Bible will stand through the last great conflict." [3]

God's plan for His last generation is that they will light up the whole world with their reflection of the character of God: by their love of God, their love for each other and even sinners, by their clear understanding and explanations of Bible doctrine and prophecy, and by their transparent honesty and carefulness in all earthly matters. In the pre-advent judgment God is carefully selecting a people who walk with Him in intimacy. He will be able to reveal to them His most important thoughts. Even amid the traumatic events of the close of earth's history these people will find joy in the presence of Jesus. They will worship God in spirit and in truth.

No careless eye can view the beauties of the Most Holy Place. But God desires to open wide its doors to the hungry, thirsty, repentant, humble seeker.

"One thing I ask of the Lord, this is what I seek: that I may dwell in the house of the Lord all the days of my life, to gaze upon the beauty of the Lord and to seek him in his temple" (Psalm 27:4).

Come in, seeking heart, come in. You'll love it here.

SUMMARY

The seventh and final step in sanctuary prayer is to enter into the Most Holy Place in heaven. This is the place of judgment, in which Jesus is completing His work of salvation for the world. This is a summary of the way judgment works in each individual life:

INVESTIGATION
- God examines my thoughts, motives, and actions (Jeremiah 17:10)
- I examine my own heart and life (Lamentations 3:40; 2 Corinthians 13:5)
- The universe examines my life (1 Corinthians 4:9; Ephesians 3:10, 11)

DISCIPLINE
- Cutting: trials, persecution, suffering (James 1:2-4; Isaiah 30:19-21)
- Healing: comfort, peace, joy (Hosea 6:1: 2 Corinthians 1:3, 4)

INSTRUCTION

- God teaches us about Himself (Psalm. 25:14; Proverbs 2:1-11)
- God teaches us about ourselves and others (Study the book of Proverbs and the teachings of Jesus)
- God teaches us doctrine and prophecy (2 Timothy 3:16, 17)
- God gives us wisdom to become capable workmen in our daily life. (Isaiah 28:24-29)

I find that the three parts of the judgment: *investigation*, *discipline*, and *instruction*, mingle together in my life, yet separating them helps me in understanding and cooperating with what God is doing for me.

It is God's plan that we dwell in the Most Holy Place continually as long as we fulfill the conditions for entrance— made simple in the seven steps of Sanctuary Prayer. Our prayers need not be worded in sanctuary language, but the steps of praise, repentance and confession, cleansing, being Spirit-filled, partaking of the divine nature through the Word of God, and praying for others in intercession—must be taken before we can fully experience dwelling with God in the Most Holy Place.

---

[1] See my book, *Practical Pointers to Personal Prayer* (Review and Herald Publishing Association, Hagerstown, MD 21740) for the story of how the story of the judgment works in my life.

[2] E. G. White, *Review and Herald*, February 7, 1907.

[3] E. G. White, *The Great Controversy*, pages 593, 594.

CHAPTER TEN

How to Please God

"And without faith it is impossible to please God,
because anyone who comes to him must believe that he exists
and that he rewards those who earnestly seek him."
(Hebrews 11:6)

Prayer is the means God has planned for most directly connecting earth and heaven. There is nothing magical about Sanctuary Prayer or any other special type of prayer. But anything that aids in understanding and cooperating more fully with God is useful. The only prayer that will ever reach heaven is the earnest, fervent prayer from a humble, repentant sinner.

Let us seek to learn exactly what God desires of us in the practice of prayer. What is it that we can do that will please God the most?

God presents us with few requirements. One Book contains the whole of His instructions for mankind. The principles portrayed in that Book are condensed into ten commands, listed in Exodus 20. And those ten commands are manifested in the life of one Man, Jesus.

God has only one basic requirement: that we love and serve Him with all our heart.

"Hear, O Israel: The Lord our God, the Lord is one. Love the Lord your God with all your heart and with all your soul and with all your strength" (Deuteronomy 6:4, 5).

Our desire for God must be so great it can be called hunger or thirst. We must be eager, earnest, intent, zealous. No other condition of the heart will gain the kingdom.

"Blessed are those who hunger and thirst for righteousness, for they will be filled" (Matthew 5:6).

The children of Israel had a problem with commitment. They were forever wandering off to investigate false gods. They had divided hearts. They seemed completely hopeless.

But God loved them so very much—they were His own children—that He gave them warning after warning. He told them through Moses that if they continued to go off after other gods, He would allow them to be captured by their enemies and taken into exile. He told them of their servitude to a heathen nation. But God assured them that in spite of the terrible prognosis, there was still hope:

"But if from there you seek the Lord your God, you will find him if you look for him with all your heart and with all your soul" (Deuteronomy 4:29).

122

It all happened just as God had foretold. The Israelites continued to wander after heathen gods, and God allowed them to be carried in captivity to Babylon. They were mistreated, persecuted, and downtrodden. They who had escaped Egyptian slavery seemed forever doomed to be slaves.

But God again sent word to them, this time through the prophet Jeremiah. God had not given up on them. His one condition of blessing was still in force:

"You will seek me and find me when you seek me with all your heart" (Jeremiah 29:13).

God's condition is still the same today: the only way we will find Him is if we seek Him with all our heart. Listen to David as he pours out his heart to God in Psalm 119:

- "Blessed are they who keep his statutes and seek him with *all their heart*" (verse 2).
- "I seek you with *all my heart*" (verse 10).
- "Give me understanding, and I will keep your law and obey it with *all my heart*" (verse 34).
- "I have sought your face with *all my heart*" (verse 58).
- "I keep your precepts with *all my heart*" (verse 69).
- "*My heart is set* on keeping your decrees to the very end" (verse 112).
- "I call with *all my heart*; answer me, O Lord, and I will obey your decrees" (verse 145).

It is no wonder that God said of David, "I have found David son of Jesse a man after my own heart; he will do everything I want him to do" (Acts 13:22).

Sanctuary Prayer can be either an open door to new dimensions in personal prayer or just another clever formula to keep us busy. It all depends upon the state of our heart. There is no value in any set form of prayer. Unless we desire Jesus more than anything in life, Sanctuary Prayer may hinder rather than aid us in our search to know God and hear His voice.

Sometimes it's hard for me to be honest about where my heart really is. But the Bible gives me a few simple tests to find out. The other morning I discovered one test as I was leafing through my Bible. My eye caught the heading "Samaria Resettled" in 2 Kings 17. I have often wondered why the Samaritans in Jesus' day were so despised by the Jews, and I thought that this portion of the Bible might give me a clue. And it surely did. But it also gave me much more than insight into Jewish life; it gave me a glimpse into my own heart.

SINGLE-MINDED, VS. DOUBLE-MINDED

The story in 2 Kings 17:24-40 relates how the king of Assyria took the majority of the Jewish people of the Israelite province of Samaria into captivity and resettled the land with people from other portions of his empire—Babylon, Cuthah, Avva, Hamath, and Sepharvaim.

These foreign people were now the permanent residents of a part of the Promised Land. They immediately set up idol worship. It displeased God to have His holy land polluted with idols, and He sent lions to punish the inhabitants. Evidently this was not just a case of one or two people killed by lions, but an epidemic of lion killings, for an urgent message was sent to the king of Assyria that something must be done about it.

"The people you deported and resettled in the towns of Samaria do not know what the god of that country requires. He has sent lions among them, which are killing them off, because the people do not know what he requires" (2 Kings 17:26).

The king of Assyria took immediate action. He found an Israelite priest who had been exiled to Babylon and sent him back to Samaria to teach the people how to serve his God. The priest set up temple services to the true God and taught the people how to worship in the Israelite way. But verses 32 and 33 comment:

"They worshiped the Lord, but they also appointed all sorts of their own people to officiate for them as priests in the shrines at the high places. They worshiped the Lord, but they also served their own gods in accordance with the customs of the nations from which they had been brought."

Verse 41 goes on to say that "even while these people were worshiping the Lord, they were serving their idols." As I read this verse, God spoke to my heart. "You are like the Samaritans. You worship Me, but you also serve your own idols."

In humility—and horror—I realized that this was true. I truly love God and serve Him gladly—which I doubt that the Samaritans did—yet I, like the Samaritans, also make provision to do my own thing. God showed me that most of my problems in the Christian walk are the result of this condition in my life. What condition is this? Serving God but also serving self.

Anyone who habitually takes time out from serving God to do anything he doubts that God would approve of—be it in the line of eating, drinking, reading, television, etc.—is afflicted with one of the worst maladies the Bible deals with. This is double-mindedness, exactly the opposite of serving God with the whole heart.

The double-minded person really doubts that God will do what He says He will do. Listen to what James has to say about this:

"If any of you lacks wisdom, he should ask God, who gives generously to all without finding fault, and it will be given to him. But when he asks, he must believe and not doubt, because he who doubts is like a wave of the sea, blown and tossed by the wind. That man should not think he will receive anything from the Lord; he is a double-minded man, unstable in all he does" (James 1:5-8).

Unstable in all he does! How that breaks my heart. To think that by my self-indulgence I prove myself to be unstable in everything I do!

But God has the antidote. It is in the covenant relationship with Him:

"They will be my people, and I will be their God. I will give *them singleness of heart and action*, so that they will always fear me for their own good and the good of their children after them. I will make an everlasting covenant with them: I will never stop doing good to them, and I will inspire them to fear me, so that they will never turn away from me. I will rejoice in doing them good and will assuredly plant them in this land with all my heart and soul" (Jeremiah 32:38-41, italics mine).

"Teach me your way, O Lord, and I will walk in your truth; give me an *undivided heart*, that I may fear your name. I will praise you, O Lord my God, with all my heart; I will glorify your name forever" (Psalm 86:11, 12, italics mine).

This is a test each of us must face. But the Bible gives us other tests as well.

Money and Possessions

"Do not store up for yourselves treasures on earth, where moth and rust destroy, and where thieves break in and steal. But store up for yourselves treasures in heaven, where moth and rust do not destroy, and where thieves do not break in and steal. For where your treasure is, there your heart will be also" (Matthew 6:19-21).

God implies that my attitude toward earthly treasures is one way to judge where my heart is. What do I do with my money and possessions? Paul has a bit to say about this too:

"What I mean, brothers, is that the time is short. From now on those who have wives should live as if they had none; those who mourn, as if they did not; those who are happy, as if they were not; those who buy something, as if it were not theirs to keep; those who use the things of the world, as if not engrossed in them. For this world in its present form is passing away" (1 Corinthians 7:29-31).

I can test only myself, not others. And no one else can test me. I have never had a great deal of money, and that has been fine, as I've been happy enough without it. But I do find that when I have finally managed to buy something that I've always wanted, it's hard for me to share it.

I remember a new couch and loveseat—the first really nice furniture we ever purchased. We bought them with money from two yard sales we held just before we moved to a new area. My children were all teenagers—old enough to take care of good furniture. We were moving into a

127

large house (each of the boys had his own room for the first time), and I was looking forward to decorating my lovely home.

Our new pastoral assignment was a beach city, and my husband was eager to start beach evangelism. Before long our new home was filled every weekend with youth from the nearby Christian college; they came to patrol the beaches for the Lord. The living room and family room were regularly covered wall to wall with sleeping bags.

I loved having the young people around. My problem was my new couch and loveseat. I didn't want oily heads sleeping against the unprotected material of my furniture. Yet how could I say that no one could sleep on the couches? Would I make them all sleep on the floor when the couches were so much more comfortable?

When we had first moved into that house we had dedicated it to God. We had told Him that we would use it for His work. It was His house. Was my furniture His furniture also?

The first night the young people were there, I tossed and turned, thinking about my new couches and those greasy heads. I debated suggesting that the young people carefully cover the arms and cushions before they spread out their sleeping bags. But did I want to risk destroying the freedom and welcome the young people felt in our home?

I discussed it with God. "Lord, this is Your home and Your furniture. The only way that I can have freedom to enjoy the young people and accept them wholly is just to turn the care of this furniture over to You. I won't even look to see if it is becoming soiled."

We lived in that house for three and a half years, and young people from the college were with us nearly every weekend. We fed them, loved them, sang with them, prayed with them, counseled them, played games with them. They brought beach people into our home and "dried" them out and fed them. Our home was headquarters for beach evangelism, and a home away from home for homesick students.

When the call came for my husband to minister at a new church, I gave my 3 ½ year old couches a good inspection. They looked just like new. God had taken good care of them.

TIME AND CONVENIENCE

I passed that test. But I have not always passed my tests. One place we lived was about 30 minutes away from the academy where I was librarian. By this time my children were off to college, and I enjoyed the quiet ride to work and home again alone. I could choose the radio programs to listen to, instead of enduring the children's music. I could stop and go shopping on the way home if I felt like it. I had a lovely feeling of freedom, with only myself to please.

One day one of the teachers came to me and told me about three children who lived near me. They were unable to come to the academy because the bus did not come near them and they had no other transportation. Would I consider bringing them?

"Oh, I couldn't," I answered. "My schedule is too varied."

I began to feel guilty. Wasn't the real reason that I didn't want to bring them with me that I didn't want to inconvenience myself?

I didn't feel good about my decision.

I noticed that the children were in school each day. I made inquiry as to how they got to school. I found that the teacher who had asked me to provide transportation for them was driving 20 miles out of her way every morning and evening in order that the children could be in church school.

I had failed that test.

Belatedly I volunteered to chauffeur the children. For at least a year I had the privilege of becoming well acquainted with them, and they were beautiful children. Too bad that the Lord had to shame me in order for me to receive His blessings. This test was not on money or possessions, but on time and convenience.

"Do nothing out of selfish ambition or vain conceit, but in humility consider others better than yourselves. Each of you should look not only to your own interests, but also to the interests of others" (Philippians 2:3, 4).

The Word of God is filled with principles by which the Christian can examine himself. If we willingly test our thoughts and actions by the Word of God, we can quickly grow into His likeness. God's plan in judgment is to reveal to us in the privacy of our prayer time our weaknesses and sins. As we relinquish these to Him, He tests us in our daily lives to see if we are truly seeking Him with our whole heart.

It is not God's desire that any be humiliated by an open demonstration of their sinfulness. Jesus deals very kindly with sinners. The Jewish leaders who brought the adulterous woman to Him were not publicly rebuked. Instead, Jesus wrote in the sand at His feet the sins of each of the men. They alone read their sins. Their guilt accomplished their humiliation. However, if we refuse to repent and confess the sins that God has repeatedly shown us, He will expose our sins to others. If public humiliation does not humble us and cause us to forsake our sins, God is forced to leave us to the results of our rebellion. (Read Deuteronomy 21:18-21 for God's sanctuary illustration of the final end of rebellion.)

WORDS AND ACTIONS

Jesus gives us one more important test:

"For out of the overflow of the heart the mouth speaks. The good man brings good things out of the good stored up in him, and the evil man brings evil things out of the evil stored up in him. But I tell you that men will have to give account on the day of judgment for every careless word they have spoken. For by your words you will be acquitted, and by your words you will be condemned" (Matthew 12:34-37).

"But the things that come out of the mouth come from the heart, and these make a man 'unclean.' For out of the heart come evil thoughts, murder, adultery, sexual immorality, theft, false testimony, slander. These are what make a man 'unclean'" (Matthew 15:18-20).

I am being tested every day as to what state my heart is in by the words I speak.

"Who has the heart? With whom are our thoughts? Of whom do we love to converse? Who has our warmest affections and our best energies? If we are Christ's, our thoughts are with Him, and our sweetest thoughts are of

Him. All we have and are is consecrated to Him. We long to bear His image, breathe His spirit, do His will, and please Him in all things" [1]

Although Sanctuary Prayer is a form of prayer planned particularly for early morning to get the day started right, the principles of that prayer reach out into the entire day. If prayer works no change in the one who prays, he might as well cease praying. If my morning prayer does not affect my words and actions all day long, it hasn't really come from my heart.

The first step in sanctuary prayer is praise to God as we enter His courts. It is only right that we should end our prayer time the same way. In fact, by the time we have spent an hour in God's presence we should be overflowing with praise to Him for His blessings.

Should we just tuck those grateful thoughts away in our minds and bring them out now and then to view in solitude during the day? Oh, no, that is not God's plan. He wants our response to Him to be revealed to others by our words.

"The Lord desires us to make mention of His goodness and tell of His power. He is honored by the expression of praise and thanksgiving." [2]

It is almost as though we practice praise in our private prayer time so that we can publicly praise Him. Praising the Lord either in a meeting, a small group, or in one-to-one conversation is as much a part of God's will for us as is prayer. This is the way that we show the world and, yes, the viewing universe how much we appreciate the great gift God has given us in Jesus. And let us always be expectant of receiving greater blessings in the future.

"Far more than we do, we need to speak of the precious chapters in our experience. After a special outpouring of the Holy Spirit, our joy in the Lord and our efficiency in His service would be greatly increased by recounting His goodness and His wonderful works in behalf of His children.

"These exercises (of testimony and praise) drive back the power of Satan. They expel the spirit of murmuring and complaint, and the tempter loses ground. They cultivate those attributes of character which will fit the dwellers on earth for the heavenly mansions." [3]

For many of us public testimony is hard to do. For years I was happy to pray in public, tell a story, or teach a lesson, but it was hard to give a spontaneous testimony of God's personal goodness to me. Often my mind would go blank, and I could think of nothing to say. I hated to be repetitious or trite, so I would just slide down in my seat (at least mentally) and hope that an embarrassing pause would not force me (the pastor's wife) to my feet.

Somehow I had not considered the passage in Malachi that says: "Then those who feared the Lord talked with each other, and the Lord listened and heard. A scroll of remembrance was written in his presence concerning those who feared the Lord and honored his name.

"'They will be mine,' says the Lord Almighty, 'in the day when I make up my treasured possession. I will spare them, just as in compassion a man spares his son who serves him. And you will again see the distinction between the righteous and the wicked, between those who serve God and those who do not.'" (Malachi 3:16-18).

But God soon called my attention to those words.

One afternoon I went visiting with my pastor husband. He had a hospital call where he alone could go in, so I remained in the car and read. The book I was reading began talking about the subject of testifying in public.

"We should not come together to remain silent; those only are remembered of the Lord who assemble to speak of His honor and glory and tell of His power; upon such the blessing of God will rest, and they will be refreshed....

"Some hold back in meeting because they have nothing new to say and must repeat the same story if they speak. I saw that pride was at the bottom of this, that God and His angels witnessed the testimonies of the saints and were well pleased and glorified by their being repeated weekly."[4]

I was immediately convicted of pride. It was true. I did like to have something new and interesting to say for others to hear. I hadn't thought about God and the angels listening, and surely not that the angels wrote down in a book in heaven the testimonies that were given, along with the names of those who gave them!

Right then and there in that hospital parking lot I determined that I would never again be left out of any opportunity to praise God in public testimony.

But God had still more lessons for me to learn about this subject:

We were living in the beach city I mentioned previously in this chapter. The students from the nearby Christian college were busy filling our church on Sabbath with the homeless youth they allured off the beaches. But Sabbath morning services were not enough for our eager Christian young people. They urged my husband to let them begin Friday night and Saturday night meetings especially for the beach people. My husband gave them his support.

In no way did these meetings resemble the traditional evangelistic services that I was acquainted with. Informality and spontaneity were far more important to these young people than a structured style. The response was terrific, and hundreds attended.

Johnny, a theology student at the college, led the song service, accompanying the singing with his guitar. He had a most engaging way of putting his right hand flatly against the strings of his guitar to stop the sound abruptly at the close of a song now and then. Then he would say, "I just can't wait any longer to tell you what Jesus did for me today," or last Wednesday or whenever. Then he would follow up with a simple story of God's working in his life. Sometimes it was about school, how God helped him to know what to study for a test; sometimes it was about his car, an ancient relic that barely got him to the meetings and back. (We eagerly awaited news of that car from night to night. It seemed to run on faith alone.) But often his testimony was about an opportunity the Lord had given him to witness to a fellow student, a service station attendant (because of the old car), or someone else he had met.

As he finished his testimony he would pause and look around at us and say, "Has God done anything special for you this week?" Of course He had, so we responded with stories of God's intervention in our lives, also. For the first time in my life I was eager to testify. The testimonies of the young people were alive and unusual. I recognized the presence of the Holy Spirit.

For me there was just one disturbing element in the whole service. One girl who came every night was the first to respond almost each time that Johnny asked, "Has God

135

done anything for you this week?" The problem was that she always said exactly the same thing: "I just want to say tonight that I love Jesus."

I was sure that I was an expert on the human heart. Often when I examined my own heart I found no love there at all! The human heart has no ability to produce love; of that I was sure. Since I couldn't even be sure of the love I had for my family with whom I lived, how could I possibly say that I loved God whom I had never seen?

I knew that God loved me with a marvelous everlasting love totally unlike my undependable human love, and I rested completely in God's love for me, not in my love for God.

"I just want to say tonight that I love Jesus." Each night I heard this testimony, and each night I questioned in my mind why she didn't recount some blessing she had received *from* God instead of claiming to be *giving* God something! I grew more and more irritated.

One night I felt I could stand it no longer. When she spoke her testimony, "I just want to say tonight that I love Jesus," I countered inaudibly with "What a hypocrite! How can she say that? How can human love ever be counted as praise by a holy God? Why can't she praise God for blessing her as everyone else does? Why can't she say she's thankful God loves her instead of that she loves God?"

Just then a sweet inward voice spoke to my heated mind. "Carrol," the Voice said, "do you believe I love you?"

"Oh, Lord," I responded immediately, "You know I believe You love me. Why, I couldn't exist a single day without Your love! The evidences of Your holy love are around me constantly!"

136

"Then why," the Voice persisted, "is it so hard for you to take some of the abundant love that I give you and return it to Me? Why do you insist that it is impossible?"

The pleading love in that Voice broke my heart. Sudden revelation flooded over me. I had thought that I was being conscientious and honest, when in fact I was only being self-righteous and prideful. I wanted to manufacture love myself, when in reality all love comes from God alone.

I jumped to my feet. At Johnny's nod, I spoke. "I just want to say tonight that I love Jesus."

Looking inward, I had seriously doubted my ability to love others. Looking upward to Jesus, I realized that the only love I had to give was from Him, and He gave freely, enabling me to love freely also. I need not stop to examine my emotions; I could just believe the promise of God and reach out to give what God had given me.

Oh, there is such a lot God will teach us if we are willing to step forward, doing what we know to do. If we will publicly praise God, not only in meetings but one to one or in small groups, God will pour out His blessings upon us.

"Our confession of His faithfulness is Heaven's chosen agency for revealing Christ to the world. We are to acknowledge His grace as made known through the holy men of old; but that which will be most effectual is the testimony of our own experience. We are witnesses for God as we reveal in ourselves the working of a power that is divine. Every individual has a life distinct from all others, and an experience differing essentially from theirs. God desires that our praise shall ascend to Him, marked by our own individuality. These precious acknowledgments to the praise of the glory of His grace, when supported by a Christ-like life, have an irresistible power that works for the salvation of souls." [5]

God likes to hear even our stumbling praise spoken in fear and trembling. It has taken me a long time to realize this, but I know that it is so.

How I long for the time when I will perfectly pass every test. That time will come, for God promises that He will complete what He has begun.

"To him who is able to keep you from falling and to present you before his glorious presence without fault and with great joy—to the only God our Savior be glory, majesty, power and authority, through Jesus Christ our Lord, before all ages, now and forevermore! Amen" (Jude 24, 25).

Perhaps now you can understand better why Sanctuary Prayer really works. It is seeking God with all your heart and soul, and seeking to know Him better. It involves putting into practice the words of God. It is learning doctrine and prophecy, but even more than that, learning love and self-control.

The place and time to begin is right where you are as you read these words. Do not worry about form and words. Just reach out to God with your whole heart.

PRAYER

No words make
prayer,
Only a heart
reaching out
to God
is prayer.

You may speak
Spanish, German,
any dialect;
God
can understand.
He made
the languages,
He made
you.

You may
express
no words,
only long
for God
to make you
wholly His.
The intensity
of your desire
is prayer.

No words make
prayer.
Only a heart
reaching out
to God
is prayer.

SUMMARY

God's one requirement for salvation is that we seek Him with our whole heart. He will not accept a divided allegiance.

The Bible gives us tests that we can apply to ourselves to show us where our heart is:

1. Single-mindedness versus double-mindedness
   a. A double-minded man is unstable in all he does
   b. God will bless the single-minded
2. Money and possessions
   a. Where your treasure is your heart will be too
   b. Your possessions are not yours to keep
   c. We should not become engrossed in the things of the world
3. Time and convenience
   a. Our time belongs to God
   b. We should put others before ourselves
4. Words and actions
   a. Every word we speak is recorded in heaven
   b. God loves to have us speak out His praise before others

No words make prayer, only an undivided heart reaching out to God is prayer.

---

[1] E. G. White, *Steps to Christ*, page 58.

[2] E. G. White, *Christ's Object Lessons*, page 298.

[3] Ibid, Pages 299, 300.

[4] E. G. White, *Early Writings*, page 115.

[5] E. G. White, *The Desire of Ages*, page 347.

Sample Sanctuary
Prayer

(Written as a letter)

My Dear Heavenly Father:

IN THE COURTYARD OF PRAISE

I come before You today, singing Your praises:
  "Who is like you—majestic in holiness,
    awesome in glory,
    working wonders?" (Exodus 15:11).

Although You are the King of the universe, yet You love me and invite me to enter Your presence today. How I praise Your name. You created the earth and everything in it. You created me. The whole universe is Yours. Your knowledge and glory are far greater than I can comprehend.

SANCTUARY SECRETS TO PERSONAL PRAYER

AT THE ALTAR OF SACRIFICE

I come by faith to the altar of sacrifice, the cross of Calvary, where Jesus died for my sins. I confess my sins before You. (Anger, pride, cowardice, lust—confess these in specific terms, such as: "Forgive me for speaking impatiently to my husband, my wife, my child.")

You have promised, "If we confess our sins, he is faithful and just and will forgive us our sins and purify us from all unrighteousness" (1 John 1:9).

May it be true of me that "1 have been crucified with Christ and I no longer live, but Christ lives in me. The life I live in the body, I live by faith in the Son of God, who loved me and gave Himself for me" (Galatians 2:20).

You died for me on the cross that I might live. I desire to offer my body as a living sacrifice, "holy and pleasing to God" (Romans 12:1). May I live for You today.

AT THE LAVER OF WASHING

I come to the laver, Lord, asking You to wash me clean. "Though your sins are like scarlet, they shall be as white as snow; though they are red as crimson, they shall be like wool" (Isaiah 1:18).

Exchange my weakness, Lord, for Your strength, my pride for Your humility, my selfishness for Your love. Give me the mind of Jesus.

I renew my baptismal vows before You today. I am Your child, and my deepest desire is to serve You and represent You perfectly in the world.

AT THE LAMPSTAND

I come before the lampstand desiring to be filled with the fullness of the Holy Spirit. You have told us, "If you then, though you are evil, know how to give good gifts to

142

your children, how much more will your Father in heaven give the Holy Spirit to those who ask him!" (Luke 11:13).

Fill me, I pray, with the sevenfold aspects of the Spirit: wisdom, knowledge, understanding, counsel, power, reverent submission, and righteous judgment (Isaiah11:1-5). May the Holy Spirit be visible in my life through the fruits of the Spirit: "love, joy, peace, patience, kindness, goodness, faithfulness, gentleness and self-control" (Galatians 5:22, 23).

AT THE TABLE OF HIS PRESENCE

"You prepare a table before me in the presence of my enemies" (Psalm 23:5). My great desire is to become a partaker of the divine nature. By studying Your words and obeying them I eat of the bread of life and You strengthen me. May the life I live today be under Your control. I wear the armor that You have lovingly provided for me as a protection against Satan and my own evil heart:

The belt of truth

The breastplate of Christ's righteousness

The shoes of the readiness of the gospel of peace

The shield of faith

The helmet of salvation

The sword of the Spirit, which is the Word of God

(Eph. 6:13-17).

AT THE ALTAR OF INTERCESSION

I come by faith to the altar before the throne of God, where Jesus continually offers up the incense of His perfect human life on my behalf. I thank You for giving me the confidence to come boldly before You. "For we do not have a high priest who is unable to sympathize with our weaknesses, but we have one who has been tempted in

143

every way, just as we are—yet was without sin. Let us then approach the throne of grace with confidence, so that we may receive mercy and find grace to help us in our time of need" (Hebrews 4:15, 16).

I come desiring that my thoughts and my words may be pleasing to You. I want to be an intercessor with You for others, even my enemies. May I forgive each of them as You have forgiven me. May my love for them enable me to intercede for them through the power of the Holy Spirit.

I bring before You today my family, my friends and neighbors, those with whom I am studying the Bible, my church leaders, members of my church, and government leaders. (Ask the Lord to give you His agape love for these people as you pray for them, by name when possible. You might divide your prayer list into days of the week to make it easier to pray.)

IN THE MOST HOLY PLACE

My Father, I come by faith to the place I long to dwell in forever, the most holy dwelling place of God. I know that this is Your place of judgment—but also that You are always wholly just and merciful. May I be willing to look into my own heart and lay it bare before You, allowing You to purify me by the fires of trial, sorrow, and suffering. May I accept trials as Your workmen preparing me for Your kingdom.

Give me ears to hear Your instruction. May I learn more and more about You, about myself, about how to love others, about Your great plans for me and for humanity. My desire today is to hear Your voice say, "Whether you turn to the right or to the left, your ears will hear a voice behind you, saying, 'This is the way; walk in it'" (Isaiah 30:21).

I go, my Father, to the duties of my day, rejoicing in the surety of Your presence with me.

I pray this in Jesus' name. Amen.

(I often sing "The Lord's Prayer" to end my prayer time.)

Dear Reader:

I have written this out to give you an idea of how to get started in actually praying Sanctuary Prayer. Singing praise songs is always a good way to begin. Hymns and choruses may be included in each of the steps.

It is not my intention that you pray exactly what I have written out as your daily prayer. Your personal prayer must come from the depths of your own heart. No one can program the Holy Spirit.

However, this sample may give you an idea of how to choose scripture and song to make your prayer time more worshipful. Your personal need and heart's desire will guarantee you a hearing. God is in the business of revealing Himself to those who seek Him with the whole heart. He will delight to whisper His encouragement to you personally through His Word and through His voice in your mind.

Jesus' admonition to the people of His day was: "He who has ears, let him hear" (Matthew 11:15). That is still God's admonition for us today.

The first prayer for each of us should be, "Lord, teach me to pray." God will answer that prayer in a most wonderful way!

SANCTUARY PSALM

Praise the Lord!
Praise Him with joyous laughter;
    praise Him with tears of contrition.
Praise Him at the altar of sacrifice;
    praise Him with cleansing at the laver.
Praise Him with the golden oil of the
    Holy Spirit.
Praise Him at the table of His presence;
    praise Him at the altar of intercession.
Praise Him in the Most Holy Place;
    praise Him for His holy law and judgment.
Praise Him for His investigation,
    for His discipline, and for His instruction.
Praise Him for each day and its blessings.
Praise Him with words and song,
    with the piano, organ, and voice.
Let my every action and every word
    praise the Lord.
    Praise the Lord!